THE CULTURE OF JAPAN
AS A NEW GLOBAL VALUE

HAKUBUN SHIMOMURA

Former Minister of Education, Culture,
Sports, Science, and Technology

IBC Publishing

The current form of Western civilization, including its implementation in modern Japan, is reaching its limit. Environmental destruction, abnormal weather, diminishing energy sources, terrorism—isn't this the beginning of the end of life as we know it? I think that we can find hints of a new paradigm to replace the current one in traditional Japan.

Humankind coexists with nature in a symbiotic relationship. I felt the truth of this age-old wisdom of Japan while visiting Ise Shrine.

The feeling of awe that comes from living together with nature, the knowledge that one may die at any moment, leads to a deep appreciation of each and every meeting with other people, which is called ichigo-ichie *in Japanese: that every meeting is a unique event that will occur only once in a lifetime. This awareness produces the politeness and consideration of the Japanese people and the Japanese ability to work together as a group, the marvelous qualities on which so many people visiting Japan have remarked.*

As human beings grow and become spiritually mature, they are able to see things that they formerly couldn't see, to see values that were formerly invisible.

A new start in life is not given you by other people; it is something that you discover and realize on your own. But once you have determined your path in life, heaven will then lend a helping hand.

To bring the diverse peoples of the world together in harmony, a certain type of leadership is needed—a leadership possessed of a deep spiritual confidence that is rooted in humility and modesty.

What the world needs now is a willingness to recognize differences as differences and a readiness to learn from others, raising one and all to a higher level of being.

Japan is a country that values vagueness, the blurring of lines between opposites. It is this that enables harmonious coexistence.

It is impossible for a Japanese to become a respected person of the world without first becoming truly Japanese. A firm foundation in Japanese soil is required for building a global edifice.

THE CULTURE OF JAPAN AS A NEW GLOBAL VALUE

HAKUBUN SHIMOMURA

Translation by Michael Brase

Front Jacket: Photograph by Katsuhiko Mizuno.
Design by Stone Bridge Press (U.S.A.)

©2016 Hakubun Shimomura, 2016 IBC Publishing, Inc.

All photographs by Katsuhiko Mizuno.

Published by IBC Publishing, Inc.
Ryoshu Kagurazaka Bldg. 9F, 29-3 Nakazato-cho
Shinjuku-ku, Tokyo 162-0804
www.ibcpub.co.jp

All rights reserved. No part of this book may be reproduced in any form without written permission from the publisher.

First Edition 2016

ISBN978-4-7946-0374-6 C0082

Printed in Japan

Contents

Preface 7

CHAPTER 1
Ise Grand Shrine: Coexisting with Nature   11

Visiting the Ise Grand Shrine   12

> My First Visit 12 • The Poet Saigyō at the Ise Shrine 14 • The Parthenon and the Ise Shrine 17 • The Japanese Spirit 19 • Overseas Visitors to the Ise Shrine 20

Japan Recovers Again and Again from Natural Disasters   23

> Is Japan a Power Spot? 23 • Coexistence with Nature Forms the Japanese Mindset 25

The Imperial Family as the Bedrock of Japan   27

> One Unbroken Imperial Line 27 • The Emperor's Occupation Is Daily Prayer 32 • The Emperor's and Empress's Heartrending Reaction to March 11, 2011 33 • The Reason for

the Longevity of the Emperor System 34 • The Emperor as the Spiritual Basis of Japan 37 • Humility: The Key to 21st-century Leadership 39 • Japanese-style Leaders 40 • The Humility that Comes from True Confidence 41

Cultural Heritage 42

Absorbing World Culture and Preserving It for the World 42 • Inheriting and Maintaining Culture 44 • A NASA Official on Technology Transmission 45 • Japanese Expertise in Tacit Knowledge 46 • The Modernist Yukichi Fukuzawa 48 • Recovering Confidence in the "Land of the Rising Sun" 50

CHAPTER 2
Kumano Shrine: World Coexistence 53

Visiting the Kumano Shrines 54

The God in the Mirror 54 • The Value of Visiting a Shrine 56

Thinking about Education at Kumano 58

Education for the New Millennium 58 • Schools Need to Change Their Thinking 61 • From Input Education to Output Education 63

The Wisdom of Coexistence 66

The Numbers Do Not Add Up 66 • Live and Let Live 68 • Vagueness: The Wisdom of Coexistence 69 • Shinto *Kami* as the Father, Buddha as the Mother 70 • Heaven Is Watching 71 • A Place Where Everything Is Seen 74

Leadership for Coexistence   75

  The World Begins to Take Note of the Importance of
  Coexistence 75 • Diversity as the Driving Force Behind
  Japan's Evolution 76 • Now Is the Time to Vocalize Japanese
  Values 78

Economics Leveraging Japanese Thought   80

  Japanese-style Capitalism 80 • The Maturing of Capitalism Is
  Spiritual Maturity 82 • From Intangible Capital to Intangible
  Economics 83 • Regional Revitalization and Japanese-
  style Capitalism 85 • Religious Culture and Japanese-style
  Capitalism 88

CHAPTER 3
Kumano Nachi Taisha   89

  Visiting the Nachi Waterfall   90

    Fenollosa and the Nachi Waterfall 90 • Lessons Learned at
    the Nachi Waterfall 92 • Feeling the Divine Presence 93 •
    Revival from Nature 94 • Nature as Other, Nature as All 97

  The Japan That the World Needs   97

    Being First and Foremost 97 • On Becoming Global 100 •
    Japanese Culture Abroad 101 • From the East to the World:
    Spreading Japanese Values 103 • Japanese Confucius
    Institutes 104

CHAPTER 4
To the Japanese of the 21st Century   105

Asia and Japan   106

Japan as a Cultural Polity 106 • East Asian Nationalism 107 • Reassessing the Tokyo War Crimes Tribunal from an Indian Perspective 108 • Is Asian Integration Possible? 110 • 2,000 Years of Japan–China Relations 111

Preparing for the Tokyo Olympics   112

Sports and the "Way" 112 • The Olympic Spirit and Japan 113 • Ichiro and the Japanese Spirit of Sports 115 • Shinto and Japanese Sports 117 • Why Are the Olympics so Enthralling? 117 • One's Rival as a Mirror of Oneself 119 • A Chance to Showcase the Best of Japan 120 • Replacing Nuclear Energy 121

A Society for the Young and Old, Men and Women   123

The Speed of Population Decline Is the Issue 123 • Rebuilding the Japanese Economy through Education 124 • New Workforces for a Shrinking Society 125 • A Multiple Career Friendly Society 126 • Acceptance of Immigrants Only a Matter of Time 128 • The Importance of Education with a Social Purpose 130 • Who Implements Social Purpose? 131

Postscript   133

About Hakubun Shimomura   137

Preface

In September 2013 I received my first invitation to the World Economic Forum (Summer Davos) to be held in Dalian, China. In between sessions I had the opportunity to hold a good number of bilateral meetings with top world leaders. One person who left a lasting impression on me was the Malaysian John Pang, a broadminded young strategy consultant who is an advisor not only to the government of Singapore but also to the governments of Malaysia and Myanmar.

One of his remarks that struck me was that "the turning point in human history that we are living through is a special opportunity for Japanese cultural leadership." While not many Japanese people concur with this opinion, I tend to agree with him, and we hit it off immediately. In January 2014 we met again at the World Economic Forum in Switzerland (Winter Davos), and that is when I began to make plans to write this book.

John Pang's wife is Japanese, which may of course be one of the reasons he is so knowledgeable about Japan, but in any event I decided, together with him, to take a closer look at how Japanese culture could have a renewed relevance in shaping the emerging world culture of the 21st century.

I believe that the Ise Grand Shrine and the Three Grand Shrines of Kumano are key to understanding Japanese history and culture, and so I began to make travel plans with John to visit these Shinto shrines from August 10 to August 12, 2014. There were to be more than 10 of us, including John's wife.

Unfortunately, on August 10, a typhoon evacuation warning was issued affecting some 500,000 people within Mie Prefecture alone, which is where the Ise Grand Shrine is situated. It seemed somewhat reckless to attempt to visit the Ise Shrine, the first stop on our itinerary, but no one in the party suggested postponing the trip. To our surprise, everything proceeded without a hitch from the outset of our trip in Tokyo. There were few train delays, and in the afternoon we were able to visit the Outer and Inner Shrines at Ise as planned.

As you read this book, I hope that it will become clear why I think that Ise and Kumano are symbolic of how Japan might play a larger role on the global stage in the 21st century.

However, I would like to stress from the beginning that this book is not intended to be an expression of ultra-nationalism or extreme patriotism. Over the course of its long history, Japan has generally held to principles developed in ancient times that prioritized world peace over national aggrandizement. As far back as the 6th and 7th centuries,

Prince Shotoku spoke of the spirit of harmony, the traditional Japanese desire to live in peace with nature and to coexist with other living creatures. It is unfortunate that in recent times the Japanese have sometimes lost sight of these noble principles.

In his documentary *An Inconvenient Truth*, Nobel Prize winner and former United States Vice President Al Gore predicted that half of the species on earth today will disappear within the next 100 years. The future for humankind does not seem promising given global warming, the depletion of energy resources, and water and food shortages.

I believe that this is the time for Japanese people to look again at our past, to benefit from the wisdom of the ancients, and to formulate a new worldview. Obviously I am not suggesting that Japan should force its opinions on other nations; this new worldview must be based on Japan's traditional cultural values of living in harmony with nature and with other human beings. I do believe that this new worldview can contribute to the international community, and it is in that spirit that I wrote this book, in the humble but very earnest desire to contribute to international prosperity.

If current policies persist unabated, pessimism about the future of humankind will grow ever more pervasive. In this book I hope to present a few ideas for consideration as to how we can prevent this from happening.

HAKUBUN SHIMOMURA
December 2015

1

Ise Grand Shrine: Coexisting with Nature

Visiting the Ise Grand Shrine

My First Visit

The Ise Grand Shrine consists of 125 shrines and other buildings, enshrining the sun goddess Amaterasu-omi-kami in the Inner Shrine and the god that protects food, clothing and accommodation in the Outer Shrine. The Ise Shrine is the most important of over 70,000 Shinto shrines in Japan.

I first visited the Ise Grand Shrine 24 years ago when I was 36, prompted by the words of one of the professors at the University of Tokyo: "The current form of Western civilization, including its implementation in modern Japan, is reaching its limits," he said. "Environmental destruction, abnormal weather, diminishing energy sources, terrorism—isn't this the beginning of the end of life as we know it? In traditional Japan I think that we can find hints of a new paradigm to replace the current one. Humankind has experienced the rise and fall of civilizations a number of times in the past. Some of what the global community needs now can be found in Japanese traditional civilization. A hint of what is needed is at the Ise Shrine. It is only by going there that you can grasp what that might be."

Guided by his words, my family and I set out for the Ise Shrine. My oldest child was three, the youngest only one, so the trip was made with baby carriage in tow.

The Ise Shrine is said to have a history of over 2,000 years. The deity enshrined in the Inner Shine resided in the Imperial Palace until the rule of the 10th emperor, Sujin

Minister Shimomura and his party walking down the pathway leading to Ise Shrine.

(97 BC–30 BC according to tradition). Thereafter, according to *The Chronicles of Japan* (AD 720), the presence of the deity proved so powerful that the emperor decided to find a better location for enshrinement, and had his daughter, Toyo-suki-iri-bime, relocate the deity to Yamato-kasa-nui-mura. During the reign of the 11th emperor, Suinin, a still more suitable location was sought, and his fourth daughter, Princess Yamato-hime no Mikoto, left Nara Prefecture and traveled through Kyoto, Wakayama, Okayama, Shiga, Gifu, Aichi, and Mie Prefectures, searching for a suitable location, before deciding on the vicinity of Ise Isuzugawa river, the present location of the Ise Shrine.

A child of the postwar Japanese education system, I had developed a negative attitude toward Japan's native religion of Shinto, and to religion in general. It had never crossed my mind to visit Ise, and the opportunity to do so had never arisen. However, as I walked up the sacred approach to the Inner Shrine, following the advice of the University of Tokyo professor, I could not help but feel that Ise was indeed a very special place.

The Poet Saigyō at the Ise Shrine

Almost 1,000 years ago, the famous Buddhist priest and poet Saigyō (1118–90) wrote the following poem when he visited Ise Shrine:

> I do not know what deity resides here,
> but my eyes water,
> feeling so blessed.

Visiting the Ise Shrine, Saigyō feels a presence; he does not know what or who it is, but he feels it nevertheless. It is the presence of a god, but it was only by coming to Ise that he was able to feel that presence. He finds his eyes filling with tears, although he does not know why.

On my first visit to the Ise Shrine, I did not feel the same subtle, instantaneous reaction as Saigyō, but I did experience a miraculous moment amid the cedar trees. Along the sacred pathways of the Ise Shrine are many cedars. In many Western nations, most likely a garden would be created here. Maybe all the trees on the approach to the shrine would be cut down, and the area would be transformed into a beautiful artificial garden. And if there happened to be a tree growing in the middle of a path, that tree might also be cut down.

At Ise, however, that tree in the middle of the path is not touched. If a cedar should be growing where a shrine building is to be erected, the roof of the building is built around it. You might ask why it is necessary to build the shrine in that spot; why not move the location of the shrine building if you do not want to cut down the tree. The reason is that the location of a shrine building is all-important, but so is the life of the tree. At Ise Shrine, it is essential for sacred structures to be built in locations of spiritual power, but if a cedar happens to be growing in that sacred spot, that cedar

The woods of Ise Shrine seen from Uji Bridge.

Kazahinomi no Miya, Inner Shrine, Ise Shrine.

is not cut down, nor is the shrine moved. The shrine is built around the tree.

The Inner and Outer Shrines of the Ise Shrine are rebuilt every 20 years, a practice that started in 690. The latest rebuilding in 2014 was the 62nd. This practice has thus been ongoing for over 1,300 years. The numbers seem not to add up because the shrines were not always rebuilt exactly every 20 years, and there have been interruptions due to civil war. During the latest rebuilding, again no cedars in the shrine precincts were felled. The trees obviously had grown larger over time, so that means that the opening in the roof to accommodate the cedar had to be made proportionately larger. Yet still, no cedars were harmed.

The Parthenon and the Ise Shrine

Throughout the world there are many ancient sites of considerable renown, such as the Greek Parthenon. Just as the Ise Shrine is devoted to the goddess Amaterasu-omi-kami, the Parthenon was originally dedicated to the goddess Athena. When Greece was invaded by Christians in the 6th century, the statue of Athena was removed and the building converted into a church dedicated to the Virgin Mary. In the 15th century, Greece was occupied by the Ottoman Empire and the Parthenon was transformed into a mosque. In the 17th century, the war between the Republic of Venice and the Ottoman Empire resulted in critical damage to the structure, reducing it to the partial ruins we see today. On the other hand, while the Ise Shrine is made of wood and thatch and built on a small scale, it has managed to retain its simple, austere appearance almost unchanged for over 1,300 years. If this is not a miracle, what else should we call it? We must thank our forebears for handing down to us the Ise Shrine in a form very close to the original, dating back around two millennia.

In its sacred precincts the Ise Shrine transmits to us a living tradition, very close to the lifestyle and religious beliefs of its original inhabitants. In the midst of its woods, the same for over 1,300 years, Ise Shrine still stands as it originally

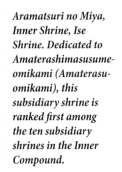

Aramatsuri no Miya, Inner Shrine, Ise Shrine. Dedicated to Amaterashimasusume-omikami (Amaterasu-omikami), this subsidiary shrine is ranked first among the ten subsidiary shrines in the Inner Compound.

stood. As Japanese it is our duty to pass on to future generations the wonderful legacy of the Ise Grand Shrine.

As I was visiting the shrine, the query posed by the university professor—"What hint for how we should live in the 21st century is to be found at Ise?"—popped into my mind. I thought, "It is the coexistence of humankind and the natural world." That is the conclusion I intuitively reached. Human beings do not exist independent of the planet but coexist with nature. The Ise Shrine is a symbol of the importance that ancient Japanese assigned to nature, seen in the towering cedar, chinquapin, and oak growing along the shrine's pathways. I feel that the fact that this simple shrine dedicated to Japan's most important deity—Amaterasu-omikami—is surrounded by forest is an expression of the modest dignity at the heart of Japanese culture.

The Japanese Spirit

As I mentioned earlier, I am a product of the postwar education system, what you might call a socialist education. While it was not explicitly stated, social studies then were taught based on a socialist view of history. And since socialism eschews religion, there was a definite tendency to deny its validity. We were taught that there are different levels of religion, and that Shinto is considered a kind of animism, the most primitive form of religion. This was not taught to us directly, but the fact that I somehow adopted a negative attitude toward religion had its roots, I believe, in this socialist worldview.

Nevertheless, when I visited the sacred precincts of Ise Shrine, I felt the ancient wisdom of the Japanese people that calls for us humans and nature to coexist in harmony. What I felt in my heart then was not respect or reverence or even joy. It was a kind of awe. It was an awe of something that was entirely beyond human control. This awe-inspiring power is, I believe, what people call "god." It is a feeling that transcends religions and religious sects, ideologies of every type—it is what flows in the blood of the Japanese people. Shinto is not a primitive religion; it is, in fact, the heart and soul of Japan. That is what I felt during my first visit to the Ise Shrine.

Overseas Visitors to the Ise Shrine

It seems that many overseas visitors to the sacred Ise Shrine are also touched in much the way I was. One day an exchange student told me he could easily tell the difference between a shrine and a park. The instant you pass under the *torii* gate at the entrance to a shrine, he said, everything is very clean and the air is pure, whereas parks seem dusty and dirty. Even though both places are replete with greenery, the distinction between parks and shrines is clear, he seemed to be saying. Needless to say, the most outstanding exemplar of this distinction is the Ise Shrine.

At 7.44 meters in height, a Shinmei torii *gate stands at either end of the Uji Bridge.*

Many famous people from overseas have visited the Ise Shrine, and left behind words that would seem to be in sympathy with that view. For instance, in the Ise Shrine guestbook the renowned British historian Arnold Toynbee wrote: "Here, in this holy place, I feel the underlying unity of all religions."

Meeting with overseas visitors is part and parcel of my current role. I hope that they will always have the opportunity to visit the Ise Shrine and experience its special atmosphere for themselves.

Uji Bridge, Inner Shrine. This wooden bridge, 101.8 meters in length and 8.42 meters in width, stands at the entrance to the Inner Shrine:. Traversing the Isuzu River at an approximate 90 degree angle, it is the symbol of Ise's Inner Shrine.

Japan Recovers Again and Again from Natural Disasters

Is Japan a Power Spot?

As I mentioned in the Preface, in the 21st century a number of threats to human existence are becoming increasingly serious, such as the issues of limited resources, energy, food, global warming, and overpopulation. It may be that the civilization that Japan has developed over 2,000 years is exactly what is needed for the world in the 21st century. I think that we need to reflect anew on our cultural past, admit where it has been lacking, revisit its merits, and regain our lost confidence.

However, in order not to repeat the mistakes of history, I am not proposing a return to the notion that the Japanese are somehow superior to other peoples. I am not saying that Japan is somehow better than other nations. You may ask then, why I say that Japanese traditional philosophy may have a greater role to play in the 21st century. One reason is the role of geography.

Just the other day I returned from Bangalore, India. Bangalore is located on a plateau about 1,000 meters above sea level and enjoys a mild climate with a steady temperature of about 20 degrees Celsius throughout the year. It is as though it were perpetually spring, making it an eminently comfortable place to live and work, an environment blessed in every way. For that reason, it has been attracting IT companies from around the world, and there is even a university dedicated to information technology. I paid a visit to the university's open campus, and found it open in more ways than one: it literally had no glass windows and no air conditioning. Without tempestuous storms or typhoons to disrupt them, in an environment not too hot and not too cold, the students are able to pursue their studies without a worry in the world. All in all, it is a wonderful place.

Japan, on the other hand, is situated in a land of extremes, visited every year by typhoons, blizzards, earthquakes, and other natural calamities. While this produces the beauty of the changing seasons, once every 100 years it also produces a disaster of such proportions that recovery seems impossible, but from which Japan, nevertheless, always fights its way back, giving us the country we know today. Japan's land area amounts to only 0.5% of the world total, yet it accounts for 20% of the world's natural disasters. This means, I believe, that Japan sits on a focal point of tremendous energy. The fact that earthquakes and volcanic eruptions occur so frequently is an indication of the enormity of this energy. It may also mean that Japan, in feng shui terms, is situated on a power spot. Japan is overflowing with energy, more than many realize, and it is said that Buddhist temples and Shinto shrines were historically built at locations where this energy was felt to be strongest.

Coexistence with Nature Forms the Japanese Mindset

Macrobiotics has recently become famous in the United States, but has existed in Japan from olden times. Michio Kushi, the founder of modern macrobiotics and a long-time resident of Boston, said that when he first went to the United States, he took with him some *kabocha* seeds (a kind of squash) to cultivate, and thereafter included *kabocha* in his diet. However, after about four years of cultivating the seeds in the United States, the *kabocha* lost its flavor. Wondering why, he found that the soil was apparently deficient in energy. America uses a lot of artificial fertilizers, but what growing plants need more than fertilizer is the energy found in the soil. Japanese soil seemed to him to possess more energy than American soil. That is why, even without the use of fertilizers, Japanese *kabocha* tasted so much better. This was the conclusion that Mr. Kushi came to, based on his own experience.

This is not limited to food alone. The whole of Japan is overflowing with energy. That energy is found within nature itself. Japanese people are not superior to other nations, but through the repeated trials and tribulations arising from Japan's harsh environment, I believe that they have incorporated the energy of nature into their worldview in a somewhat different way from that of other countries. In contrast to Bangalore's pleasant situation, in Japan you may lose your life in the next disaster, you may lose your home and fields, you may be unable to plant crops for the coming year. Over many generations of living under such conditions, the Japanese people have learned how to coexist with nature and how to survive. At the same time, because of the unpredictable, ever-present danger of calamity, the Japanese have come to understand and appreciate the transience of life.

The feeling of awe that comes from living together with nature, the knowledge that one may die at any moment, leads to a deep appreciation of each and every meeting with other people, which is called *ichigo-ichie* in Japanese: that every meeting is a unique event that will occur only once in a lifetime. This awareness produces the politeness and consideration of the Japanese people and the ability to work together

Farmer working in the rice paddies near Matsuzaka City, Mie Prefecture.

as a group, the marvelous qualities on which so many people visiting Japan have remarked. In recent memory, these traits were demonstrated in the aftermath of the terrible tsunami of March 11, 2011, when there was almost no civil unrest, no looting or pillaging; the disaster victims went quietly about their lives with great dignity, scenes that were widely reported by overseas media.

The Imperial Family as the Bedrock of Japan

ONE UNBROKEN IMPERIAL LINE

Although the subject of the Japanese imperial family can be considered controversial, I believe that the imperial family is key to understanding Japanese philosophy and history, and the Japanese worldview. In understanding how Japan should contribute more to the world, therefore, I think it is necessary first to understand more about the history and role of the imperial family and what it means to Japan, and to see what lessons may be learned from an institution that has survived for so long. It is in the same spirit of humility I mentioned above that I wrote the following section, and it is my earnest desire that the reader might come to understand the imperial family from a Japanese perspective, covering the whole course of Japanese history, not just recent history.

Japan is considered to be the oldest extant country in the world, which many in Japan believe is the result of the single unbroken line of the Japanese imperial house. The imperial house traces its roots back to Amaterasu-omikami, the very deity that is enshrined at Ise.

In addition to the energy derived from nature, Japan as we know it today is obviously the result of the growth and development of the nation over many, many generations. The way for us in Japan to express our gratitude for this achievement is for the Japanese people to consider how Japan can best contribute to the global community.

It is not clear that the meaning and significance of the imperial house to Japan is widely understood overseas, and even in Japan there are not many chances for the Japanese people to grasp its true meaning. In order for Japan as a developed country to play a more meaningful role on the world stage, I think it is necessary to create opportunities for people abroad to learn more about the meaning and significance of the emperor system, and thus to deepen mutual understanding. For that reason, I would like to spend some time in this book delineating the system's essential features.

According to the 8th-century *Chronicles of Japan* and *Records of Ancient Matters*, Japan's two oldest recorded histories, Amaterasu-omikami, the chief deity in the heavenly plains known as Takamagahara, sent her grandson Ninigi

Looking up from the path leading to the Inner Shrine, one sees a kaleidoscope of leaves and light.

to Takachiho in Kyushu to pacify and rule over the rice-rich country of Japan. This is the origin of the imperial house.

Thereafter, leaving Kyushu to conquer the east, the sixth in line from Amaterasu-omikami, Kamu-yamato-iware-biko-no-mikoto, assumed the throne as the first emperor, Emperor Jimmu, at Kashihara in Nara Prefecture in 660 BC. This marks the birth of the imperial line and of the Japanese nation, with the present emperor being a direct descendant of Emperor Jimmu.

Among the present 29 hereditary monarchies in the world, the Japanese imperial house is the oldest surviving continuous hereditary monarchy.

The British royal house has changed seven times since the Norman Conquest. The present House of Windsor traces its direct history back 300 years to George I, who assumed the throne after the House of Stuart, to which George I was related, failed to produce an heir, coupled with the added complication of religious considerations.

It is often said that China as a state has a history of 4,000 years. It would also be possible to say that the long history of the Chinese state is the sum of the shorter histories of the surnames of the changing ruling houses. The first Chinese emperor, Qin Shihuang, assumed the throne in 221 BC, some 2,200 years ago. In China, it was permissible to replace the emperor when the "mandate of heaven" was lost. Thus, within the same country many different peoples strove against each other for hegemony, and when a dynasty changed, all the members of the previous dynasty were eliminated, and the culture that had prevailed until then was brought to an abrupt halt. The name of the age was changed to that of the name of the new imperial house. For example, the ethnic members of the Han dynasty had the surname Liu, and the Sui dynasty, founded by the Xianbe, a northern nomadic people, had the surname Yang. The Yuan dynasty was established by a member of the Mongolian Borjigin clan. The Qing dynasty was founded by the Manchurian Aisin Gioro. Thus, with a change of dynasty, the surname of the ruling family changed, and the name of the age changed also.

In Japan, by contrast, the imperial lineage is unbroken, and the imperial family, in fact, has no surname. The given name of Emperor Showa was Hirohito, that of the present emperor Akihito, and that of the crown prince Naruhito, but in actual fact these personal names are never used; rather titles are made use of when referring to members of the imperial family. The fact that the imperial family has no surname is an attestation to its continued unbroken heritage.

The emperor of Japan is a human being like everyone else, and the symbol of the state, but the emperor is also the ethical cornerstone of the country, performing Shinto rituals and other spiritual functions. The fact that the imperial family adheres to the highest standards of conduct and self-discipline is one reason it continues to earn the respect of the people.

The Emperor's Occupation Is Daily Prayer

Thus we can see that Japan is a country that has preserved and protected its imperial lineage, but not a country where the monarch himself rules over the nation. The emperor is not a political authority but rather the fount of cultural authority, perhaps somewhat like the current system in the United Kingdom, where the queen reigns but does not rule. In olden times, the emperor referred to his subjects as "the emperor's treasures" (*omitakara*) and reigned over their well-being. This relationship of mutual trust means that in Japanese history we do not see usurpers rise up and attempt to overthrow the throne, as so often happened in many other countries. Over its history many powerful warlords rose to dominance in Japan, but while they ruled the country and some even received the title of shogun, or supreme military commander, they never threatened the position of the emperor.

This is not widely known, but the emperor's principal occupation is prayer. The emperor continually prays for the peace and happiness of the people. The emperor's travel plans can be learned from the newspapers and elsewhere, but the nature of his prayers is entirely unknown. The emperor is the head Shinto priest of the nation, and prays every day for the nation's peace and stability. He does this not for himself but for the people. His existence is a living Japanese tradition. In a sense, the emperor does not live for his own sake but for the good of the nation and its citizens. It is this that causes him to be respected in the eyes of the people; it is this that lends him his spiritual authority.

The Emperor's and Empress's Heartrending Reaction to March 11, 2011

In the aftermath of the Great East Japan Earthquake of March 11, 2011, the people in the afflicted areas had reached the limits of human endurance. Over 200,000 people suffered the ultimate in hardship and deprivation, having lost their homes and often their families and living in temporary quarters in high school gyms and other such places. The sight of the Emperor and Empress traveling to the distressed areas almost immediately afterwards was extremely moving. Seeing the disaster victims sitting on the floor, the imperial couple themselves knelt down, lowering themselves to the same eye level, and they talked with each person one by one, offering words of compassion and encouragement. In their position as Emperor and Empress, they could not offer material relief, but they could offer words of sympathy and encouragement. Hearing the words of the Emperor and Empress, each person spoken to could not help but be moved to tears. Other victims who were not in attendance but watching elsewhere on television were affected in the same way, as were indeed people in Tokyo. These scenes are still fresh in people's minds today.

While watching television, I remember the tears welling

up in my eyes when Empress Michiko said to one of the victims, "I am so glad that you survived." As words of consolation from one individual to another, I can think of nothing more profound. These words were not uttered by a superior to an inferior but were an earnest expression of happiness at the other's well-being, demonstrating the inimitable and miraculous power of words.

Japan is blessed with an emperor and empress, and an imperial family, who continually pray for the happiness and peace of the people, demonstrating in themselves the highest standards of conduct and self-discipline. It is because of these figures that the Japanese people are able, even in the most arduous conditions, to remain composed, to appreciate the help of others, and to endure. It is this unseen power, what you might call an exalted power, that makes the imperial family a special entity, and it is that entity that forms the basis of what is remarkable about Japan.

The Reason for the Longevity of the Emperor System

While it is true that the emperor system has existed for 2,000 years, not every emperor enjoyed the same absolute security and invulnerability. Looking back over history, it occurred to me that one person who might have successfully displaced the emperor was the 16th-century warlord Oda Nobunaga, who laid the foundations for the political reunification of Japan after a long period of civil war. With that thought in mind, I visited the ruins of Azuchi Castle, Oda Nobunaga's final residence. Azuchi Castle was excavated some 30 years ago, and watching the video of the excavation, I saw that next to the castle's central tower was a building dedicated solely to entertaining the emperor. That would suggest that even the preeminently powerful Nobunaga had no intention of displacing the emperor. While it is true that he was planning to abolish the Ashikaga military government of the time, he had not the slightest intention of becoming emperor himself. It was unthinkable to him to overthrow the emperor system that had formed the very foundation of the country for so many hundreds of years.

I think that the fact that Japan is an island nation has also been a factor in the longevity of the imperial house. That is, there are geographic obstacles to invasion by other nations. In the Nara period (710–794), extant records show that there was a growing fear of continental invasion, and military outposts were established from southern Kyushu all the way up to the Nara region. However, Emperor Shomu believed that these outposts might not be enough to protect the country, and that the greatest safeguard would be a tightly knit nation that prayed and worked together as one body. Thus he issued an edict for the creation of a great Buddhist statue in which everyone could participate. He himself became not a figure of political power but a symbol of authority, who first and foremost prayed for the happiness and peace of his people.

Subsequently, successive emperors reigned for the

purpose of praying for the well-being of the state, rather than ruling over their subjects. If the emperor had remained in a position of political power, somewhere along the way there would have been an attempt to topple the emperor and for someone else to take his place. Ultimately the people's reaction to any powerful ruler is an underlying feeling of fear. No matter how complacent the people may appear on the surface, their primary motivations are fear and self-gain, which results in a society that cannot be called peaceful. This is precisely why Emperor Shomu made a distinction between ruling and reigning, creating a system in which the emperor became the fount of authority but did not rule himself.

However, a potential danger to social stability arises when this fount of authority is raised to the level of a god. To prevent this from happening, the imperial family has adopted a stance of supreme modesty and humility in regard to its position, never forcing its authority unwillingly on its subjects. One reason the emperor system has continued unbroken for so long lies in its profound knowledge of the meaning of authority.

The existence of the emperor system met its most serious threat in the aftermath of World War II, when Japan was occupied by the Allied forces. The occupying forces' supreme commander, General Douglas MacArthur, was inclined to abolish the emperor system, but when he met Emperor Showa he was so impressed by the emperor's character that he changed his mind. Emperor Showa, however, was not the only member of the imperial family to have a laudable character; in fact, the institution of the imperial family itself seems to create such people. It is because the emperor and other members of the imperial family do their utmost to carry out their duties to the people that the imperial family has survived for so long.

The Emperor as the Spiritual Basis of Japan

If the emperor system had been abolished after World War II, Japan might not be enjoying the prosperity it does today; such is the extent to which the imperial family forms the spiritual bedrock of the nation. If there were no emperor, this bedrock would disappear. While ordinary Japanese may not be fully aware that the stability of their lives depends on the existence of the emperor, it is nonetheless true that because of this bedrock the traditional values of Japan continue to thrive. Furthermore, it is also because of this bedrock that the Japanese people can respond flexibly to other cultures and incorporate other cultures into their lives.

Naturally, it is not feasible for every country to have an emperor system, and each country must establish its own foundations according to its own history and traditions. The important thing is for each country to have a firm understanding of its roots, and in the case of Japan, that means to protect and preserve the emperor system, the product of its ancient history, its view of nature, its traditions.

The fact is that there are many countries in the world that

have had their cultural legacies cut short, or have forgotten or abandoned them. Even in Europe there are no countries with histories of several millennia, since all have been subject to invasion or conquest or even mass migrations. There are virtually no countries that have maintained the same regime for more than 2,000 years. The second longest in the world is the Danish royal family, with a history of about 1,000 years; most of the other dynasties have histories of a few hundred years. From a world perspective, a history of more than 2,000 years is almost miraculous, which is all the more reason for Japan to cherish the imperial institution.

The role of the emperor is like that of a chief priest. His role is to pray for the peace and happiness of the nation, and

Minister Shimomura signs the official Ise guestbook.

for that reason he has come to be loved by the people—an extraordinary case in world history. The Japanese people should be thankful for this remarkable history, and based on that they should seriously consider how Japan can contribute to the international community.

Humility: The Key to 21st-century Leadership

When we look at the emperor and imperial family, we are looking at a symbolic version of Japanese-style leadership. Japanese-style leadership can be expressed in the following words: "To lead a thousand people, you must bow your head to a thousand people."

Which is to say, if you are the chief executive of a company with a thousand employees, you must be prepared to bow your head to a thousand people in humility and appreciation. And if you are the head of a country of 130 million people, you must be prepared to bow your head to 130 million people with humility and modesty. This, plainly put, is the essence of Japanese-style leadership.

There is something akin to warmth and benevolence in the words and conduct of the members of the imperial family. This is entirely different from the feeling emanating from a person possessing political power like a shogun. A future emperor, who is one day to reign over the nation, is educated from his early years to care for the people; he comes to possess a humility and appreciation of others, sentiments gently enveloped in love and affection. This can be transmitted without the need for words. Looking about the world today, where one power clashes with another, one cannot help but feel that this type of Japanese leadership has something important to teach us about the sort of leadership for which the 21st century should be striving.

Japanese-style Leaders

We hear much about Western styles of leadership that focus on procedure: "What can I do to exercise stronger leadership?" or "What should I do to be more persuasive?" The traditional way of Japanese thinking is quite the opposite. In Japan, the thinking is that the person who can mentally join hands in earnest prayer with his companions will naturally be given the role of leader. For example, the great Buddhist priest Shinran (1173–1263) had many followers, but is said to have taken no disciples, since he considered all believers to be his companions in the search for truth. As we can see from this, the philosophy of leadership in Japan has depths of which we can be proud. In the 21st century, when many countries come together to coordinate their activities in a harmonious way, I think that it is increasingly this spirit of leadership that is needed.

The renowned clinical psychologist Hayao Kawai, who also served as the chief of the Agency for Cultural Affairs, once described Japanese leadership as an "empty center structure." The Japanese leader, the more excellent his or her qualities, reduces his presence to such a point that you would think him not a leader at all. Standing near such a person, you might think he lacked leadership qualities, but at the same time you would sense that he had something special about him, something that can bring people together, some power that is not superficially apparent. This is the paradoxical world of Japanese leadership. Leaving aside the question of whether such a superlative leader exists in Japan today, the Japanese idea of a leader contains the profound notion that the ultimate goal of a leader is to efface his role as a leader.

The Humility that Comes from True Confidence

Those of us engaged in politics have often been indirectly criticized by people who say that Japan as a nation has lost confidence in itself. Having been involved in government and foreign affairs for several decades now, I can admit that there may be some truth in this argument. In the end, however, the roots of Japan lie in the words of Prince Shotoku (572–622) who, when addressed by the emperor of China as the sovereign of Wa (Japan), replied proudly that he was "the prince of the land of the rising sun." Japan is such a country, combining both humility and self-confidence.

The aforementioned Hayao Kawai said that "human beings cannot be truly modest if they do not have true confidence." This applies not only to individual human beings but also to nations. If you do not have confidence in the culture, the philosophy, and the morality of your own country, you lose all sense of humility and tolerance, and are unable to accept the culture, thinking, or morality of other nations. If you do not have confidence in the values of your own country, you feel threatened when confronted by the values of other cultures. On the other hand, if you have true confidence in the values of your own country, you can accept those of other countries and learn from them with a sense of humility. There is the catchphrase "Japanese spirit, Western technology," which was popular when Japan was first setting out on the road to modernization in the Meiji period (1868–1912). These words imply a fundamental confidence in the Japanese spirit. This is the confidence that allows one to accommodate the ideas of other cultures, without the fear of losing one's own spiritual roots. This is not the Western type of confidence that says, "I am strong," but a confidence backed by true humility and national pride.

Cultural Heritage

Absorbing World Culture and Preserving It for the World

In April 2015, the ASEAN Ministers Responsible for Culture and Arts (AMCA) and the AMCA Plus Three held a meeting in Hue City, Vietnam, which I attended. After the meeting, all 13 participating nations staged presentations of performing arts from their country. The Vietnam national broadcasting system provided two hours of live coverage, with each country allotted about 10 minutes of performance time. All of the countries except Japan were represented by what seemed to be their top pop-culture artists, most of them beautiful young women who sang and danced. The one exception was Japan, which was represented by performers whose average age was over 70. The group was the Nantogakuso, performers of classical court music (*gagaku*) which has a history dating back many centuries. The members of this group could not be called young, but in my opinion they had greater stage presence than that of the other performers.

Why was this performance so impressive? The reason is that it was performed in a form unchanged since the 8th century—in the same way, in the same costumes. *Gagaku* was first brought to Japan by a Vietnamese Buddhist priest. *Gagaku* is thus a Vietnamese art, but it has survived only in Japan. Modern-day Vietnamese have little knowledge of its history, and the art has died out in Vietnam.

This is one example of many arts and crafts that have entered Japan, been subjected to a process of selection, then been internalized and become a part of Japanese culture. What made this possible was the fact that the basic regime of Japan has not changed. In China, on the other hand, despite its over 4,000-year history, the present People's Republic of

China is only 70 years old, and unfortunately many relics from 4,000 or 5,000 years ago have been lost. Conversely, Japan is a repository of many performing and fine arts that have died out in their country of origin.

Inheriting and Maintaining Culture

Geography has played an important role in making this possible. Japan is situated in the extreme Far East, so that it is the last stop for world cultural assets flowing from West to East. While Japan welcomed these cultural treasures, it did not pass them on across the Pacific, but melded them with its long cultural tradition, creating something new without supplanting its historical legacy.

The Ise Shrine is the paramount example of this process of renewal. As mentioned earlier, the shrine is rebuilt every 20 years. The new shrine is a replica of the old one, built on the adjoining lot. This rebuilding allows for the transmission of craftsmanship from one generation to another, and for the meticulous preservation of an immemorial cultural site. This periodic rebuilding, coupled with the making anew of the many artifacts kept in the shrine buildings, also requires the education and training of a wide variety of artisans. Without this ritual rebuilding, the cultural lineage of Japan could not have been maintained, and 1,300 years of history would have been lost.

This method of creating a structure to maintain our

culture, and not allowing the line to be broken, can, I think, be called typically Japanese. To my mind, what made this possible is again the imperial family. Without a solid foundation at the heart of the country, the acceptance of outside influences can lead to confusion and a loss of direction. But Japan had the imperial family to provide that foundation. The present emperor is the 125th in line from Emperor Jimmu, forming an unbroken line that is the bedrock underlying Japanese life. The imperial family is the backbone that has made more than 2,000 years of uninterrupted history possible.

A NASA Official on Technology Transmission

I recently came across a somewhat contrary example to this in a talk given by a NASA official. NASA succeeded in sending a man to the moon some 45 years ago, but now, he said, even with all the technological advances that have been made since then, it could not be done that easily today. The reason is that the requisite technology and know-how accumulated at the time of the last voyage has not been transmitted to the current generation. Of course, with all the gains made in computer science and in other areas, it might be possible in, say, 10 years' time, if they began again from scratch, but he said that it could not be done tomorrow, because the technology had not been passed on.

In Japan, on the other hand, the transmission of technological expertise has been going on for countless generations. This can be viewed as a miraculous occurrence in Japanese history, or even in the annals of world or human history. It is something the Japanese can be proud of, and which we should make known more widely throughout the world, not just as a technological matter but as something intimately intertwined with civilization itself. Now, with the world facing one dire crisis after another, I believe it is even more important that these facts be widely disseminated.

Japanese Expertise in Tacit Knowledge

This gives rise to the question of why the Japanese are so good at transmitting knowledge from generation to generation. One reason is that the transmission of skills involves a type of knowledge that cannot be put into words, that is, tacit knowledge. The West has tended to stress knowledge conveyed by the written word, whereas in the East in general and in Japan specifically the focus has been on knowledge that cannot be put into words, knowledge that is passed directly from one person to another.

In Zen Buddhism, for example, the interplay between master and disciple is an attempt to transmit untransmittable knowledge. In this exchange, the master never tells the disciple the correct answer. The master proposes a riddle that is virtually impossible to unravel, and the disciple racks his brains trying to solve it. Through this process, the master tries to lead the disciple to a place where enlightenment can take place. Zen speaks of "not relying on the written word," which we can take as referring to tacit knowledge, and "just sitting," which means that just practicing meditation in itself can lead to this knowledge.

When the professor at the University of Tokyo encouraged me to visit the Ise Shrine, he was teaching me to answer the questions "what is Shinto, what is the spirit of Japan, what

Sitting on the veranda of the Kaguraden, Minister Shimomura and John Pang look out on the courtyard garden while discussing world affairs, Asia, and Japan.

is Japanese civilization?" not through a reliance on words but through the acquisition of tacit knowledge, the result of actually visiting the shrine.

Taking this a step further, we can say that Shinto itself is a religion of tacit knowledge. Shinto has never developed a theoretical framework, and from the perspective of theologically rich Western religion, Shinto could be seen as being devoid of substance. But, in fact, it is precisely because Shinto transcends theory that it has not developed an ideological framework. It may be that the 21st century will finally come to understand why Shinto is the way it is.

The Modernist Yukichi Fukuzawa

Of course, not all Japanese have been proponents of tacit knowledge. Take, for example, Yukichi Fukuzawa (1835–1901), who could be called the father of modern Japan, and whose portrait appears on the 10,000-yen banknote. As a child he is said to have visited a Shinto shrine expecting to see a god inside, but when he saw nothing, instead of leaving a coin in the collection box, he left a stone. This led Fukuzawa to deny the validity of Shinto, thinking it nothing but a folk religion not based on anything concrete.

Fukuzawa was one of the driving forces behind the 19th-century modernization of Japan. He believed that Japan lagged behind the West and that in order to modernize, Japan should assimilate Western science with the utmost speed. Given the times, and the fact that Western industry was at the core of the West's economic success, Fukuzawa's viewpoint was timely and meaningful. However, the world has changed, and it would seem that there are limits to this worldview. While Fukuzawa's thought process is not without merit, the people of the 21st century will not be able to transcend the limits of Westernization and modernization unless they acknowledge the important things in this world that are invisible and tacit.

As human beings grow and mature spiritually, they are able to see things that they formerly could not see, to grasp values that were formerly invisible. As a child, Fukuzawa thought that if he looked inside a shrine, he would see something, that god was something that could be seen. But with spiritual maturity, human beings realize that even if there is nothing to see superficially, there may be something that exists beyond the physical reality. Being spiritually undeveloped, children are likely to think that the only things that really exist are the things that can be seen. That is why, I believe, it is important to teach children at an early stage in their education that there are important things in this world that are invisible to the naked eye.

In his later years Fukuzawa said that the difference between Buddhism and Christianity was like the difference between green tea and black tea, that the differences were not really that significant, and the important point was whether you enjoyed the flavor or not. He went on to make comments to the effect that religion had an important role to play in society. He had finally come, I think, to realize the importance of what is invisible to the naked eye.

Recovering Confidence in the "Land of the Rising Sun"

Surviving the Meiji period, when Yukichi Fukuzawa lived, and enduring the years of the Pacific War, we are now marking the 70th year since the end of the war. This postwar era constitutes, I believe, an abnormality in the long history of Japan. It was during this period that, due in part to Allied policy, the view of Japan as an invader and as a misguided country was overemphasized, when national pride and confidence was lost, and when the destruction of the Japanese spirit began. After the bursting of the economic bubble and the ensuing so-called "lost decades," Japan then lost confidence in its economic prowess and has essentially been wandering in the dark. From a social point of view, incidents are now occurring almost on a daily basis that would have been unthinkable from a traditional Japanese moral perspective. Diplomatically, there was also a period when Japan offered repeated apologies for the war. What Japan now needs to do is to shake off this feeling of uncertainty, recover its former sense of pride, and contribute to world peace.

Japan may be a small country, but it has always had pride in itself. In AD 607, responding to a missive from the emperor of Sui, Prince Shotoku wrote in answer, "From the sovereign

Sunrise over Toba Bay, Mie Prefecture.

of the land of the rising sun to the sovereign of the land of the setting sun," enraging the Chinese emperor by his apparent arrogance. This incident in no way indicates that Prince Shotoku was unaware of the fact that the Sui dynasty was immeasurably larger and more powerful than Japan. Far from it, the prince was fully cognizant of the superlative nature of Sui culture, and, in fact, was one of its most avid students. However, no matter how small Japan might be, it was not a Sui tributary, and Japan showed this pride and sense of independence in its diplomatic relations. What is needed now is for Japan to regain that pride and spirit.

2

Kumano Shrine:
World Coexistence

Visiting the Kumano Shrines

THE GOD IN THE MIRROR

I always encourage people who are visiting the Ise Shrine or traveling in the Kumano region to also visit the three shrines of Kumano: the Kumano Hongu shrine, the Kumano Hayatama Shrine, and the Kumano Nachi Shrine. I believe that these three shrines are the best place to experience with all of the five senses the culture which Japan has developed over its long history. To get to Kumano from the Ise Shrine, you must cross the border from Mie Prefecture into Wakayama Prefecture, and even though it is a considerable distance, you will, without fail, understand why I encourage visiting these shrines once you have arrived in the Kumano region.

At the Ise Shrine, only prayers for the peace of the nation or the world are considered appropriate, whereas at the Kumano shrines one is also allowed to make personal prayers. One point of particular interest, and not seen in many other places, is the large mirror hanging in front of the main worship hall, which visitors face as they pray. As you may know, mirrors play a particularly important role at Shinto shrines.

There is a significant play on words associated with mirrors that I would like to mention here. The word for mirror in Japanese is *kagami*. The *ga* in the middle of the word can be taken to mean "the self" or "the ego," and if this is removed, the result is *kami*, which is the Japanese word for "god." With a little imagination, we can see that the mirror is a suggestion that if we rid ourselves of our selfish ego, each of us can become one with god. This is the reason for the mirror in the shrine. God is you yourself; you yourself are god.

The special spaces afforded by shrines are, in fact, more numerous in Japan than any other country. If you have the

Minister Shimomura answers questions on the bus from Ise to Kumano.

opportunity to visit one of these shrines, you may experience some kind of revelation. The Kumano Hongu Taisha is commonly believed to be a place of revitalization and of new beginnings, but this does not mean that a new life is given by heaven or by other people, but rather that you yourself discover what is needed for a fresh start. The purer of heart, I think, are more likely to make these discoveries.

The Value of Visiting a Shrine

Still, I think that most people visit shrines because they are seeking help or succor, or in order to overcome some difficulty in their life. In that sense, the Great East Japan Earthquake and the tsunami of March 11, 2011, taught the Japanese people an important lesson. Up until then, they had a roof over their heads, they had a home, they had futons to sleep on, they had three square meals a day—these were all taken for granted and not particularly appreciated. However, after March 11, these things came to be seen as blessed gifts, not only by the victims of the tragedy but by all Japanese. Electricity was another one of the givens of everyday life, but even that turned out not to be guaranteed.

Faced with a natural disaster of this scale, people may visit a shrine for spiritual consolation. When they do, they may experience spiritual growth. When faced with tribulation, people may visit a shrine for inner healing, and when they do, they may feel a deeper spirituality. Shrines are special spaces like this, and when people have this type of experience, they tell their friends and relations, and the number of people partaking in this valuable experience grows. For overseas visitors too, it is good to enjoy Japanese cuisine or to go shopping in Tokyo, but you might have a more fulfilling experience if you visit shrines such as those at Ise and Kumano. It might provide the opportunity to look within yourself. In that sense, Japanese shrines and temples can be counted among the sacred places of the modern world.

On my most recent visit to Kumano, I had the strangest feeling as I stood in front of the main hall. It was as if my

The Kumano region, often referred to as "the place on the other side of the mountains," is 90% forest.

spirit had left my body and entered the sacred structure, literally an awe-inspiring moment.

Thinking about Education at Kumano

Education for the New Millennium

Since Kumano was registered as a World Heritage Site, the number of school excursions visiting the area has apparently increased. In Japan as a whole, however, such excursions to temples and shrines are said to have dwindled. This is a pity, since experiencing the tranquil atmosphere of these sanctuaries would be an event of the utmost value for young students.

Not too long ago the mathematician Masahiko Fujiwara published a best-selling book called *The Dignity of the Nation*, in which he touches upon the conditions required to educate gifted students. The first condition is that the student be brought into contact with the beauty of nature.

Present-day education in Japan might be called input education, the goal of which is to stuff as much information into the brain as it can possibly hold, focusing on the powers of memorization and rote learning. True enough, in order to inculcate the skills needed for an industrial society in the 20th century, it was important to learn European thought

Hayatama Shrine, one of the three Kumano shrines.

and to strengthen the left side of the brain. In today's world, however, now that Japan is one of the most developed countries in the world, just learning from the West is no longer a guarantee of success or even progress. In a sense, Japan has lost its main objective, which had been to overtake the West. We no longer live in an age where our goals and vision for the future are set by the West, and all we have to do is implement them. What is important now is the ability to create our own vision for the future, to set our own goals, and to solve the problems and issues now facing us.

This means that input education is no longer sufficient; what is needed is "output education." The English word "education" literally means to bring or lead out. Output education thus brings out the best in children's imaginative and creative faculties. It is here that the spiritual space of a shrine or temple can play a part. By providing children with the opportunity to visit these special places, one also provides them with the chance to expand upon their inner capabilities. It is also beneficial to their emotional and aesthetic education.

It is often said that what we need is education that fosters the creative and imaginative powers of students, but in more cases than not, this type of education stops at the level of problem-solving. I believe, however, that education involving visits to shrines and temples can truly bring out these qualities at a much deeper level. Particularly for young students, coming into contact with, and experiencing, the beautiful and the spiritual in life can help them realize their innate potential.

Schools Need to Change Their Thinking

Many school teachers may have reservations about this proposal. What concerns them is that having students offer a prayer at a shrine might be construed as forcing on them a particular religion. That is not my intent; my intent is to have the students experience a spiritual space that is steeped in history and tradition. A recent trend is for student groups to be given free time before even entering the *torii* gate of the Ise Shrine, with the question of whether or not to pray being left up to the individual student. Thus, many students visit neither the Inner nor Outer Shrine, but simply buy a souvenir at one of the shops and leave. This is a shame, for they have squandered the opportunity to visit a very special place.

Not only in Japan but in all advanced countries, the 20th-century input style of education was highly successful in bolstering our modern industrialized society. Anyone educated in that way could find employment and play a meaningful role in society. In that sense, input education was very successful and therefore has historical significance. However, the leading countries of the 21st century have developed beyond the modern industrialized society in favor of a knowledge-based society. In such societies, anyone educated in the old way will be unable to contribute to society or actively participate in it. The reason is that, with the advent of the Industrial Revolution, society required workers who could supply quick answers to answerable questions; that is, personnel well drilled in conventional problem-solving.

Knowledge-based societies, on the other hand, require workers who, with imagination and creativity, can supply answers to unanswerable questions; that is, creative thinkers. Modern Japanese education may be able to develop the conventional faculties of its students, but it is not educating creative thinkers. This is why a fundamental reform of the teaching profession is needed.

Another important factor in modern education is self-esteem. Among the nations of the Organization for Economic Co-operation and Development (OECD) which were

Minister Shimomura and John Pang on the pathway leading to Hayatama Shrine, with two cloud plumes rising into the sky behind them like ascending dragons.

surveyed for scholastic performance, Japan ranked number one for elementary and junior high school students, but when first-year high school students in four countries including Japan were surveyed (along with the US, Korea, and China), 84% of Japanese students answered in the affirmative when asked whether they thought of themselves as being incapable or somewhat incapable. This was by far the highest figure for the four countries surveyed. In other words, Japan may be the best at cramming facts and figures and developing the conventional mental faculties of its students, but the competition among students promotes a feeling that they are falling behind others, and thus fails to foster a healthy sense of self-esteem or happiness.

From Input Education to Output Education

I am not denying, of course, that there is value in education that encourages the acquisition of knowledge and the promotion of intellectual performance. However, what must be provided by school education from here on, I believe, is more opportunity for self-discovery and self-realization. If that cannot be done, young people will spend the rest of their lives thinking they are incompetent. To prevent this unhappy state of affairs, conventional education has to be radically reformed.

There are three skills that must be nurtured. First is the initiative to solve difficult problems on one's own. Second is

Minister Shimomura and, to his left, John Pang and Kumano Hongu Chief Priest Ietaka Kuki.

the creativity to resolve an extremely difficult problem with an innovative solution. Third is the ability to be able to work as one with others with warmth and kindness. In the present educational system, these qualities cannot be acquired, no matter how hard students apply themselves to mathematics, English, or the Japanese language. The most formidable task facing Japanese education today, not to mention the other advanced nations of the world, is how to teach these skills.

As a matter of fact, it has only been in the last 150 years or so that Japanese education has focused on cramming facts and figures into the heads of its students. It was different before that. By referring back to how things were done in the past, perhaps we can glean some insightful ideas for the 21st century. One idea, as mentioned earlier, is to provide young people with the opportunity of experiencing shrines and other wonderful places steeped in history. This may stimulate their desire to live a fuller life.

These days, whenever I visit shrines during the summer vacation, I do not see many children playing there. In the old days you would see children running around the shrine precincts, perhaps with a cage in their hands looking for cicadas or dragonflies. The shrine grounds were cool, and they felt like an extension of one's own garden. Nowadays children stay indoors playing video games, and I get the feeling they have forgotten how to have fun out in nature. As for grownups, in the past maybe once or twice a year they would go to a festival at the local shrine, buy things at stalls set up in the precincts, and catch up with their neighbors. Temples and shrines used to serve this function. It would be nice, I think, if these spaces could be put to greater use again.

The Wisdom of Coexistence

The Numbers Do Not Add Up

Here I would like to digress, to tell an interesting story about the Kumano Shrine. In Kumano there are actually three shrines: Kumano Hongu Taisha, Kumano Hayatama Taisha, and Kumano Nachi Taisha. The three together are referred to as Kumano Sanzan. The deity enshrined in these shrines is called Kumano Gongen. In ancient times, monks and nuns would travel around the country using pictures to explain about belief in the deity Gongen to the common people, and many Kumano subsidiary shrines were built around the country.

There are said to be some 3,000 of these subsidiary shrines still standing today, but to which of the Kumano Sanzan are they subsidiary? On noticeboards at the Hayatama and Nachi Shrines, each is said to have some 3,000 subsidiary shrines, and Kumano Hongu is supposed to have the same number. Since one sub-shrine cannot be subsidiary to all three main shrines, the numbers do not add up.

Thinking this strange, about 10 years ago I checked to see how many Kumano shrines there were in Itabashi Ward,

Minister Shimomura offering a prayer and paying official respects at Kumano Hongu Shrine.

Tokyo, where I live. There turned out to be 12 or 13. So I went around to each one and asked the head priest which of the Kumano shrines it was subsidiary to. A number said Kumano Hongu, with two or three saying Nachi Taisha. The rest said they were not sure. Naturally, from such a small survey as this one cannot really draw conclusions, but it would seem that most of the Kumano shrines throughout the country are subsidiary to the Kumano Hongu Taisha.

Live and Let Live

Naturally, although it is not really necessary to decide which is ranked first, second or third, one is tempted to think that, in the West, there might have been a power struggle to settle the matter, resulting perhaps in the recognition that Kumano Hongu was the main shrine, with the Hayatama and Nachi Shrines being subordinate to it.

The three shrines have existed amicably side by side for over 1,500 years, with none submitting to the others. This is an example of Japan's live and let live philosophy, in which even if one shrine thinks it is the main shrine, it doesn't insist that the others are subsidiary shrines and dispute with them at every opportunity. Rather they have existed side by side, each prospering in its own way, for over 1,500 years, demonstrating the wisdom of mutual tolerance.

One might criticize this type of thinking as irresponsible or wooly, but from a Japanese perspective it allows everyone to live peacefully together. It does not denigrate the other party. If you decide decisively that one of the three shrines is the main shrine, the position of the other two becomes untenable. Rather than that, the three shrines have left the lines separating them blurred, allowing them to coexist. In that sense, the three Kumano shrines are, I believe, symbolic of Japan.

Vagueness: The Wisdom of Coexistence

Japanese people are very fond of this type of ambiguity, which allows people to coexist. We prefer not to define things in black or white. The same applies to the business realm. For example, titles like Assistant to the Division Director are often created for convenience's sake, leaving some to speculate that the title was given as a sort of consolation prize to someone who had failed to become a department head, though no one would state that in so many words. The person appointed Assistant believes sincerely that it is his duty to support the Director, and he has been told as much by upper management. Frontline managers believe sincerely that they have full responsibility for their departments. Everyone thus has a role to play. Japan treasures this type of ambiguity in human relationships. The fact that Japanese do not usually announce who is in charge, or who they work for, is part of this ambiguity.

In the 21st century, I believe that ambiguity will become

ever more important. Many of the world's problems cannot be resolved by thinking in black and white terms, and attempts to force a resolution may end in regional conflict or war. The Japanese way of thinking, to value ambiguity and in doing so to allow for coexistence, is not naive or wooly thinking but one wise way of dealing with seemingly insurmountable problems. In the present-day world, with its mountains of pending problems, Japan has a responsibility to stress the importance of ambiguity; otherwise there would seem to be little hope for the seven billion people on the planet to live in peace and harmony.

Despite the wisdom of ambiguity in general, I believe that the judgment as to when to leave things vague and when to make things clear is one that can only be answered by a mature civilization. Immature cultures tend to make clear what should be left vague, thereby aggravating the problem. Fundamentalism is a typical example of this failing, and, in fact, can be seen as the exact opposite of peaceful coexistence.

Shinto *Kami* as the Father, Buddha as the Mother

On a noticeboard within the grounds of the Kumano Hongu Shrine are the words: "With *kami* [Shinto gods] as the father, and Buddha as the mother." When reading these words, Japanese people feel a great sense of comfort. The thought itself seems to be a legacy of the traditional theory of *honji-suijaku*, in which Japanese Shinto gods were seen as manifestations of Buddhist deities, obviating the need to define oneself as a follower of Shinto or Buddhism. As Buddhism grew in influence in Japan after its introduction in the 6th century, the eight million native Shinto gods came to be redefined as manifestations and embodiments of Buddha. Thus, the Shinto god enshrined in Kumano is the temporary manifestation of Amida Buddha. I think that this is a good example of the wisdom of ambiguity, which deters religious conflict based on doctrinal differences.

The situation seems to be quite different in the United States. For example, if you stop at a hotel, you will find a list of local churches on the wall. They are listed by denomination, so that hotel guests can decide which church they want to attend. While this kind of categorization is definitely one aspect of religion, I cannot help thinking that if you pay too much attention to small differences, you will lose sight of the big picture. Would it not be better to surmount denominational differences and stand in simple devotion before the divine, irrespective of doctrinal differences? Japanese people tend toward a broadminded, open attitude to religion.

Heaven Is Watching

Returning to the issue of making black and white distinctions, when one person is reprimanding another in Japan, you rarely hear the words, "Don't do that. It's against the law." In Japan, deciding what is right or wrong, black or white, by

A view of Kumano Hongu Shrine showing the main hall, the Shinmon gate, the Suzumon gate, and the Mizugaki fence.

The Wakamiya sanctuary, dedicated to Amaterasu-omikami.

The Musubi no Miya sanctuary, where the gods Fusumi and Hayatama are enshrined.

appealing to the law is not common. Japan is a culture of what is beautiful and what is shameful, more than being a culture of crime and punishment. For example, when admonishing a subordinate, the boss may say, "That is really shameful." Or "The way you're going about this job is not beautiful." The question of what is shameful or beautiful is left to the conscience of the person in question, to be decided by inner dialogue. To many Westerners, this may seem ambiguous and make them feel ill at ease, but to Japanese people, this ambiguity provides the opportunity for growth and improvement.

My grandmother used to sum up this philosophy in the following way. She was basically not well educated, working in the country on a farm, but from the time when I was a small boy, she concisely expressed this culture of shame with the words "heaven is watching." The issue was how you should act when heaven was watching, not whether something was legal or illegal, whether other people were watching or not; it was a matter of how you should act when heaven was watching. As young as I was, I grasped that since heaven was always watching, I must lead a life that was not shameful in the eyes of heaven, or the eyes of the Shinto gods or the Buddhas. It was not only my grandmother who said this, but practically everyone else back then. This thinking was taken for granted at the time. The fact that it has disappeared constitutes one of the problems facing Japan today.

A Place Where Everything Is Seen

There are times when, in a religious setting like a Shinto shrine or a Buddhist temple, I have the feeling that my life is an open book. This may indeed be the feeling that "heaven is watching," but either way this is one of the wonderful things about visiting sacred places. It is wonderful not because it is a place where prayers might be answered, but because standing in the presence of something greater than yourself, you feel that everything about you is transparent—Amida Buddha is quietly watching. The critic Katsuichiro Kamei said, "The greatness of the Buddha comes from the fact that Buddha can see everything."

This is the same for Shinto gods; they see everything, but there is no judgment entailed. Having the feeling that everything about us is transparent, that there is nothing to hide, our hearts naturally take a turn toward the better in life. The power present in such places is highly valued in Japan, and throughout the East.

Leadership for Coexistence

THE WORLD BEGINS TO TAKE NOTE OF THE IMPORTANCE OF COEXISTENCE

Visiting the Ise Shrine and Kumano, I came to appreciate again the roots of Japan. Japanese people traditionally have a deep sense of coexistence and a wish to live and let live. Prince Shotoku called this the "spirit of harmony," and I think that it is important for Japanese people to understand this at a deep level as being quintessentially Japanese. Ise and Kumano symbolize this spirit, and are thus places where the Japanese spirit of coexistence may most easily be experienced.

How many nations on earth have this deep commitment to coexistence? Unfortunately, it appears that humanity today is not committed to living together peacefully. The history of humanity has been one of conflicting points of view and irreconcilable claims to righteousness. This led to the belief that converting the ignorant to one's way of thinking was justifiable. Examples of this attitude can be found in the history of Christianity. Christians believed that their religion was the consummate religion, that their beliefs were the most just, and that by spreading these beliefs they would be working toward world peace.

However, human values cannot be measured by a common yardstick; the world is replete with diverse ways of thinking. It is not that I wish to repudiate Christianity, and I realize that, in our globalized world, Christianity is itself evolving. What I wish to say is that if you try to force your own values on others, there will inevitably be conflict and war. Surely it is time to realize that such one-dimensional thinking is not going to work.

Diversity as the Driving Force Behind Japan's Evolution

However, it is not enough for different values simply to exist independently side by side. It is only when different value systems actively learn from one another that they can be said to be coexisting, allowing for each system to evolve and deepen. Japan, of course, has its traditional values, but that does not mean that it refuses to entertain values other than its own. Rather, Japan has actively and flexibly accepted what is good from the outside world. Japan has always actively accepted variety. In current jargon this would be called diversity. When people possessing different values come together in constructive discussion and collaboration, a new set of values is born and innovation occurs. I think it is precisely this process that will become ever more important to the international community in the coming decades.

It is fair to say, I think, that Japanese culture is one of the more liberal world cultures. Japan is polytheistic, as can be seen from its eight million Shinto gods and its adherence to the liberal and theistic Mahayana School of Buddhism. Christianity and Islam, on the other hand, are monotheistic, regarding their god as the only god and their religion as the preeminent religion, which gives rise to the desire to convert nonbelievers. Needless to say, this stance is far removed from the acceptance of diversity, and is one reason for the conflict between countries possessing different value systems. It is my belief that countries like Japan, which have historically been more accepting of diversity, will play an important global role in the future.

The principal reason for war in our globalizing world is the unacceptance of others. For example, Islam is opposed to and in conflict with Western Christianity in the Middle East.

The **torii** *gate leading to the site where ritualistic observances were once held at Kumano Hongu Shrine.*

There are only two possible outcomes in such conflicts: either one side emerges victorious and the other is annihilated, or both sides are annihilated. However, to the Japanese way of thinking, the fruit of a long history, there is no need for one side to meet with annihilation, for in the Japanese way neither side is repudiated, both sides recognize the other's position, and peaceful coexistence becomes possible.

In this regard, it is interesting to note that the Buddhist itinerant preacher Ippen achieved enlightenment at Kumano Hongu, a Shinto shrine, and shortly thereafter founded the Buddhist sect known as Jishu. That a Buddhist sect can be born in a Shinto shrine epitomizes this acceptance of diversity. There is a Buddhist temple standing side by side with the shrine buildings at Nachi Kumano. The enshrining of deities from two different religions in the same location might be peculiar to Japan. A senior monk at Todaiji temple in Nara once commented that, for Japanese people, Shinto and Buddhism are like the two legs of the human body, both essential to life. The heart of the Japanese philosophy of coexistence is to include everyone, to raise everyone up, and in doing so to give birth to and foster something new.

Now Is the Time to Vocalize Japanese Values

Of course, elucidating these Japanese values does not mean that we should try to impose them on the world. That would be a contradiction, given that the views we hold so important are the acceptance of diversity and the embracing of coexistence. However, I do believe that the very existence of the human race depends on the wider acceptance of such values.

The time when we could delude ourselves into thinking that resources are unlimited is over. The destruction of the environment continues apace, global warming is accelerating, and the climate is changing on a global scale. All of these phenomena are man-made, and it is clear that the human race must change its way of living if it is to survive. Here in Japan we have learned how to coexist in a world with limited resources and limited space. This knowledge is the result of a long history of living with few material resources and in cramped conditions on small, highly populated islands. As a case in point, during the Edo period (1703–1868), the city of Edo (now Tokyo) was one of the world's few eco-friendly cities. I believe Japan should now take the lead in disseminating this environment-friendly wisdom of coexistence throughout the world.

However, this leadership should not be the type of Western leadership that has pervaded the world to date, which seems to tend toward, "We are right, so do what we say." Japanese leadership is based on an acknowledgment of differences in thinking and a humble willingness to learn from others. I believe that what the world needs now is more of this type of leadership.

Economics Leveraging Japanese Thought

Japanese-style Capitalism

In the field of economics as well, Japanese thinking is perhaps more in need than ever before. We can see that the American style of extreme capitalism based on financial capital has limits, without even having to cite the 2008 financial crisis triggered by the bankruptcy of Lehman Brothers. I think that what is needed is a more Japanese style of capitalism, which stresses harmonious coexistence and the principle of live and let live.

According to the Japanese way of thinking, a commercial enterprise exists not only for its shareholders but also for its employees, its customers, and society itself. Generations of Japanese enterprises have held that the ultimate mission of a company is not just to increase profits but to contribute to society through its business. This has been the axiom to which Japanese managers have traditionally adhered. Further, the idea that profit is not the ultimate goal, but one measure of a company's contribution to society, is indicated in the following axioms: "Profit is measured by a company's social contribution" and "The greater the profit, the more of that profit must be used to contribute to society."

This type of thinking has a long history, as can be seen in the saying of Eiichi Shibusawa (1840–1931), "An abacus in your left hand, the *Analects of Confucius* in your right," and in the words of the founders of the Takashimaya department store, "What is good for the seller is good for the buyer, and is good for society," or again in the motto of the Sumitomo family, "Don't pursue quick profit."

Furthermore, this concept that work should contribute to society is implicit in the etymology of the Japanese word for "work" (*hataraku*), which is said to be a combination of the words for "others" (*hata*) and "make easy" (*raku*), thus producing "to make things easy for others." Again, in the Japanese workplace, you often hear, almost as a matter of course, the words, "For the good of other people, for the good of society at large," showing that the idea of work being a means of creating a better world is still alive and well.

It is my belief that Japanese-style capitalism, based on this view of business, profit, and labor, is bound to attract more attention in the coming years.

In fact, the world is already focusing more on this view of social contribution, profit, and labor. For example, the concept of corporate social responsibility (CSR), which arose following the Enron and Worldcom scandals, has grown in influence not only in making enterprises more aware of their social responsibilities but also of their social contribution. Moreover, in addition to entrepreneurs starting new businesses to make a profit, there are also new social entrepreneurs who aim to contribute to society or effect social reform, a growing trend taking place under the name of social business.

The Maturing of Capitalism Is Spiritual Maturity

In addition to social contribution, Japanese-style capitalism also lays stress on intangible forms of capital.

After the 2008 financial crisis that followed the bankruptcy of Lehman Brothers, many people around the world felt that a more mature form of capitalism was needed. However, nobody had a concrete idea as to what form a more mature capitalism should take. Consequently, when, for example, ideas for reforming capitalism are discussed at the Davos forum, what results is a rather low-level debate, with one side suggesting tighter regulations and the other side arguing that stricter regulations would limit free competition.

If you would like to know what mature capitalism is, I think it is necessary to answer the question, "What is spiritual maturity?"

The answer to this question is simple. Spiritual maturity means to value intangible things like wisdom, deep human connections, the trust of other people, social reputation, and the fellowship of people in an organization or a society. It follows, then, that if spiritual maturity means to honor these invisible values, then mature capitalism means a capitalism that ascribes value to invisible capital.

The next question is, what is invisible capital? It is exactly what I just mentioned. The wisdom possessed by people is called intellectual capital. Connections between people is called relational capital; the trust of other people is trust capital; brand capital is what we define as social reputation;

and the fellowship of people in an organization or society is termed empathy capital. All of these together can be called cultural capital. This cultural or intellectual capital has long been valued in Japanese-style capitalism and management, as evinced by such common expressions as the following:

> "Three people coming together have the wisdom of Manjusri [the bodhisattva of transcendent wisdom]."
> "There is something providential about this [our meeting]."
> "All thanks to you."
> "It's mutual, I'm sure."
> "Heaven's vengeance is slow but sure."
> "The public eye never blinks."

On the other hand, the type of financial capitalism that gave rise to the 2008 financial crisis stresses the tangible capital of currency, and it can be called an extremely immature form of capitalism in that its sole goal is the acquisition of money through increasing profits and rising share prices.

From Intangible Capital to Intangible Economics

Japanese-style capitalism not only ascribes great value to intangible capital but also to intangible economics.

What, then, is intangible economics, which is also referred to as the voluntary economy? Conventional capitalism is based on the idea that economic activity should produce financial reward in a monetary economy. In contrast, economic activity that is carried out for goodwill and without expectation of financial reward is called the voluntary economy. For example, housekeeping and childrearing, as well as home education and the care of the elderly at home, is largely unpaid and part of the voluntary economy. The same is true for local clean-up activities, neighborhood safety, and other community services.

In anthropology, a voluntary economy is also called a gift economy, and its history is older than that of exchange or monetary economies; in fact, it is the oldest type of economic activity in human communities. It is this intangible economy that has supported society throughout history, to the extent that tangible (monetary) economic activities would be brought to a halt without it.

In Japanese-style capitalism and business management, the voluntary economy also plays an important role in the workplace. For example, it is the custom for more senior employees to make an earnest effort to educate their subordinates as a means of repaying the senior employees who educated them. This self-effacing action is a wonderful example of voluntary economics.

Such voluntary economic activity gives birth to rich cultural capital in the areas I mentioned earlier: intellectual, relational, trust, brand, and empathy. It is within the intangible economy that cultural capitalism comes to life and begins to flow. Unlike financial, real estate, and physical capital, cultural capital is not diminished by gifting it to others. If you give intangible capital to someone, by its very nature it returns to you manifold. For example, if you give someone good advice, you develop good relations, build trust, enhance your reputation, and create empathy. For this reason, Japanese-style capitalism, which has historically stressed culture capital and embraced voluntary economics, is perhaps the economic model most suited to this era of intellectual capitalism that so many advanced economies now face.

Regional Revitalization and Japanese-style Capitalism

Japanese-style capitalism must play a significant role in the revitalization of Japan's struggling regional economies. It is not enough to rely solely on monetary economic policies and shower the regional economies with money, building more factories and ramping up employment. Intangible capital—intellectual, relational, trust, brand, and empathy—must be developed to create a voluntary economy in which the local population works in tandem with financial aid, since without a strong voluntary economy, revitalization by itself makes little progress. Conversely, when revitalization is implemented as I suggest, it can lead to the revitalization not only of local regions but also of the economy of the entire country.

Intangible capital and the voluntary economy are not

exclusive to Japan, but can still be found thriving in many developing and newly emerging countries. When the West attempts to support the economic development of such countries, its help is generally based exclusively on the paradigm of a monetary economy. The result is often that the intangible capital of these countries is lost and their voluntary economies are destroyed.

Myanmar, which has long had close relations with Japan, is a very good example of this. Being largely free of the influence of Western capitalism until recently, due to a long period of military rule, Myanmar is rich in intangible capital such as interpersonal relations, trust, and empathy. However, in the two years since Myanmar opened its doors to the world, Western capitalism appeared on the scene, and now everything has a price tag on it—land, labor, lumber, precious stones, resources such as natural gas—and the country is slowly turning into a monetary economy.

Looking at this situation, I cannot help but think that learning from Japanese-style capitalism would result in a healthier form of economic development for Myanmar.

As the Minister of Education, I didn't have many opportunities to speak about economics, but if I had the chance at the annual Davos forum, I would like to speak about Japanese-style capitalism and its focus on cultural capital, with slides behind me showing the luscious cedar trees along the approach to the Ise Shrine or the magnificent compound of the Kumano Shrine.

A place where life is renewed and fresh starts are made.

Religious Culture and Japanese-style Capitalism

When the concept of CSR, which we mentioned earlier, is discussed in the West, the words corporate compliance tend to come up. In the West this most often refers to corporations not breaking the law, but in Japan it tends to have a deeper meaning.

This is expressed in the phrases mentioned earlier, "people are watching" and "heaven is watching." Japanese culture is not a culture of crime and punishment like the West but a culture of shame and beauty. This means that the Japanese refrain from doing something not just because it infringes on the law but because other people and heaven are watching. I think that this way of thinking is increasingly in demand in a world where the law alone is failing to control the excesses of capitalism, and would, in fact, result in a more mature form of capitalism.

In this sense, Japanese-style capitalism can be said to have a profound philosophical base, integrating religious sentiment and feeling. I cannot help but think that Japan has an important role to play in the search for a more mature form of capitalism in the 21st century.

3

Kumano Nachi Taisha

Visiting the Nachi Waterfall

Fenollosa and the Nachi Waterfall

In contrast to our visit to the Kumano Hongu Shrine, which was blessed with clear skies, it was stormy when we arrived at the Nachi Waterfall. Ordinarily, the waterfall is apparently divided into three streamlets, but when we stood before it, it was roaring down in one large powerful stream, beating on the rocks below. Feeling the magnificence of the scene before me with all of my senses, I considered the significance of my being there.

In the late 19th century, during the Meiji period, the American Ernest Fenollosa, who would later exercise great influence on the world of Japanese art, visited the Nachi Waterfall. At the time many Europeans did not think highly of Japanese religion, considering it to be backward and primitive. However, Fenollosa, seeing the falls, is reported to have said this must indeed be the embodiment of a deity. This was the first time that a Westerner had recognized Japanese religion, and Japanese at the time were delighted.

Nachi Waterfall, an object of worship at Kumano Nachi Shrine. At 133 meters in height and 13 meters in width, it is the largest waterfall in Japan.

While I think that Fenollosa must have been a highly sensitive and perspicacious man, it is also true that almost anyone seeing the divine beauty of the falls must surely feel the implicit presence of a deity. And the divine presence is felt not only in the falls but in every small detail of nature there. This is the lesson, I feel, that the Nachi falls teaches us.

Lessons Learned at the Nachi Waterfall

The wonderful thing about artists is that they can recognize the sublime beauty in things that ordinary people do not see, and then give expression to that beauty. In the case of the Nachi falls, one does not need to be an artist, or have the sensitivity of an artist, to recognize and be moved by its divine beauty.

In fact, to come in contact with nature, and be moved by it, teaches us that what appears to be ordinary in everyday life is, in a sense, extraordinary, and that which appears to be plain and unexceptional is actually miraculous. It also makes us aware that the ordinary lives we lead are surrounded by a divine world. Humankind must recognize that, in order to overcome the diverse problems that it faces and to have continued existence, this awareness of the divine presence in life lies at the heart of coexistence.

My Asian friend who accompanied us to the Nachi falls said: "Standing in front of the waterfalls, I get the irrepressible feeling that the gods are living things. Before the falls, hatred, war, etc. seem irrelevant. I now realize that what is sought by the worship of nature and by Shinto is an awe-inspiring sacred beauty. That is why Japan's unique culture of beauty will surely have a beneficial impact on the world."

Feeling the Divine Presence

In his book *Uchu kara no kikan* (Return from Space), Takashi Tachibana follows the lives of astronauts after their return to earth. Some continued on as astronauts, but others, as if they had been awakened to a new truth, decided to lead a religious life. Rusty Schweickart was one of those who saw life in a new light. He said that he felt the presence of god when he went into space, but that it was not the god of any one religion; rather he felt that everything that surrounded and enveloped him was god. During a space walk, for a short period of time his connection with the spacecraft was lost and he was left tethered in pitch-black soundless space; it was then that he saw the earth suspended in the darkness, and he felt something akin to a divine revelation. After returning to earth he threw himself into religion. It seems that this feeling is not limited only to outer space. When one is alone in a desert, for example, cut off from all human contact, one is likely to feel a divine presence.

In fact, that was the feeling I experienced when standing in front of the Nachi falls. I am sure that many people feel the same. This is not the same as nature worship. Rather the waterfall allows us to feel a divine presence through the beauty of nature. It enables us to experience a divine revelation; it is not that the waterfall itself is a divinity.

Revival from Nature

The Kumano Nachi Taisha has been located in the same place since the 4th century, and people have made the pilgrimage there throughout its long history. Many have experienced a religious awakening and gone on to lead new lives. Kumano is known for its power to cause spiritual awakening, but it is not possible to put into words exactly what that experience is like. After all, it is not a matter of logic, but rather has to be experienced directly. Perhaps that is why Shinto has no verbalized ideology and why it is so difficult to grasp.

Three years ago a typhoon hit Nachi Taisha, and some buildings in the rear of the precinct collapsed and were rebuilt. It is through such natural disasters that many Japanese come to the realization that life is transient, unstable, and subject to constant change.

It was the same after the Great East Japan Earthquake. Even though Japan has become one of the most advanced and prosperous countries in the world, when faced with the sheer power of nature, we could only feel the smallness of human beings and shed tears. And we know that there will be more earthquakes. A Nankai Trough earthquake could happen tomorrow. An earthquake centered directly under Tokyo

Yoshino-Kumano National Park, known for its extraordinarily heavy rainfall.

The pilgrimage route along the Kumano River.

may occur any day. Even setting aside natural calamities, it is clear that the earth cannot continue for long on its current track. Consider the food and water shortages, regional conflicts, and the other problems facing the globe. This cannot go on forever. Something must be done. Many Japanese share this sense of crisis.

Just as astronauts, having gone through the extraordinary experience of space flight, were awakened to a new view of life, the Japanese people, experiencing the Great East Japan Earthquake and the superhuman power of nature, have awakened to a new perspective on life. Given this, is it not the duty of Japan to sound a warning?

Kumano Nachi Shrine sanctuaries in a vermilion-hued gongen-tsukuri *style, seen against the background of its tutelary mountain.*

Nature as Other, Nature as All

The Japanese have never believed that they could control nature. In contrast, the Western scientific approach assumes that human beings can mold nature to suit their needs. While it is true that the Japanese have adopted Western scientific ways of thinking, they have never harbored the thought that, amid the harsh vicissitudes of natural change, they could bring nature under their control; rather they have adopted a humbler approach, seeking to find their place in the natural order. In that sense, the Japanese do not believe in the concept of "coexisting" with nature. To coexist with nature would mean that human beings and nature are placed on an equal footing. The Japanese, rather, consider nature as being all-encompassing. That is, human beings are simply a part of nature, one part of the natural order. This is the decisive difference between the Japanese and the Western perspectives.

The Japan That the World Needs

Being First and Foremost

When I asked the head priest at the Kumano Hongu, why the three Kumano shrines had not merged, I was struck by his being unable to provide an answer. The reason he could

Minister Shimomura, with his party, offering a prayer and paying his official respects at Kumano Nachi Shrine.

A sacred dance (Dragon Dance) performed at Kumano Nachi Shrine.

not is that they had never had any intention of doing so. While each shrine has continued to claim that it is the first and foremost Kumano shrine, they have nonetheless coexisted amicably down to the present day. This is a wonderful thing in itself, but what is even more wonderful is that the three shrines never even considered conglomeration.

This story is symbolic of how we could change the world in the future. Each shrine is magnificent in itself and each considers itself preeminent, but none thinks of disputing and warring with the others to decide the matter. They are not thinking of unifying or conglomerating. Rather, while recognizing the validity of the others' existence, but still claiming to be the foremost Kumano shrine, they live side by side in coexistence and co-prosperity. The wisdom of this symbiotic relationship is something that Japan should convey to the rest of the world.

Each of the three Kumano shrines claims to have some 3,000 subsidiary shrines, but what most Japanese do not know is that most of these subsidiary shrines are overlapping. The Nachi Shrine and the Hongu Shrine each claims nearly 3,000 subsidiaries. This could be called "pure nonsense," but it is not: it points to the wisdom of how the world can build a society based on coexistence. The Japanese must delve further into the nature and wisdom of Japanese coexistence and share its findings with the world.

On Becoming Global

As indicated by the above example, the fact is that the Japanese people do not know much about Japan. They do not know Kumano, and they do not know Ise. In order to work side by side with people of diverse value systems in an increasingly globalized society, it is first necessary for the Japanese people to have a solid foundation in what it means to be Japanese, to know more about Japan. It is my hope that Japanese young people will become active on the global stage having built such a foundation. And what I mean here by "global" is not a purely American-style globalism but a Japanese-style globalism that recognizes different cultural values.

Thus, in order for a Japanese to become a global person, he or she must first become truly Japanese. Without such a foundation, he or she will be unable to win the respect of people abroad. And what I mean by "truly Japanese" is not someone who has memorized facts about Japanese history,

Minister Shimomura talking with John Pang in front of the second torii *gate leading to the shrine.*

culture, and religion, but someone who has discovered their significance for all humankind and their value for the 21st century.

Through my recent trip to Ise and Kumano I discovered a wonderful value system, a system that could make a contribution to the world. In the coming decades it is our duty, as Japanese, to convey this way of thinking, spirit, and culture to people overseas. Since most of these values have their roots in Shinto, it is necessary to convey something of the Shinto worldview. However, what is important is the Shinto worldview, not the religion itself.

Japanese Culture Abroad

In May of this year I met with former Prime Minister Mahathir bin Mohamad in Malaysia. As part of its Look East policy, Malaysia has sent 15,000 exchange students to Japan, and following the meeting with the former Prime Minister, I met with the heads of the alumni associations for these former exchange students.

Although the meetings with the Prime Minister and the alumni representatives were separate, they told me the same thing. They said they would like to see Japanese universities come to Malaysia and conduct classes in Japanese, not English. By learning from Japanese teachers in the Japanese language, they hoped to gain a deeper knowledge of Japanese culture. They told me that if they were taught in English, they would not come to a true understanding of Japan. Hearing this, it struck me forcefully that this was the true meaning of Look East.

In strictly academic terms, perhaps American and European universities would be able to teach at a higher level. But what the Malaysians wanted from Japanese universities, they said, was to be taught authentic Japanese culture in the Japanese language. They wanted to be taught etiquette, deportment, the Japanese feelings of empathy, sympathy, and concern for others. The Japanese spirit was so marvelous in so many ways, they said, and that is what they wanted most earnestly to learn.

When I met former Prime Minister Mahathir, I said that I assumed he had given up on his Look East policy. After all, the Japan he had wanted to learn from when he formulated the policy was the Japan of the past. The Japanese culture of that time had disappeared 20 or 30 years ago. With the influx of Western influence, the culture and spirit that Japan could be proud of had vanished, I thought. Japan was no longer in a position to teach the values of the past. That is why, I said, I thought the Look East policy was no longer viable. The Prime Minister told me that that was not the case. He said that Malaysia had much more to learn from Japanese culture than from Western thinking based on the assumption of white supremacy. He said that there was still a great deal to learn from Japan, and he hoped a Japanese university would come to Malaysia and conduct classes in Japanese.

FROM THE EAST TO THE WORLD: SPREADING JAPANESE VALUES

The story was pretty much the same when I visited Myanmar. In order to build a stronger economy, the country needs more technically-trained students, such as those produced by Japanese technical schools providing five years of integrated education. They want Japan to establish such a school system in Myanmar. One of the reasons they gave was that Japanese technical schools teach not only technical skills and knowledge but cultural accomplishments as well—what it means to be a human being. That's why, I was told, Myanmar needs educational institutions like Japanese technical schools, to foster solid technicians who are also outstanding human beings. I was told the same thing when I visited Vietnam.

Thus it became clear to me that one of the missions for Japan in the 21st century was to make the best of Japanese thinking, spirituality, and culture available to the rest of the world, starting with ASEAN countries. The people of Southeast Asia struggle to preserve their cultures and identities in the face of rapid economic development. They sense that traditional values that they too recognize and hold dear are well sustained in Japan. They look to Japan as a model for preserving traditional culture while pursuing economic development.

I visited New Delhi, Hyderabad, and Bangalore in India, and at each place was told they wanted to learn Japanese and have a Japanese language school established there. Of course, establishing such a school requires money and personnel, and therefore cannot be lightly undertaken. But since I was told the same thing wherever I went in Asia, I decided the matter called for serious consideration.

Japanese Confucius Institutes

This is an area where Japan can learn from China. The Chinese government has established Confucius Institutes in over 2,000 locations all over the world. Even though they are called Confucius Institutes, they do not teach Confucianism or about Confucius; rather they teach the Chinese language and promote the image of China to the world. In other words, this is part of a national strategy to boost China's global influence.

Unfortunately, the Japanese government has no strategy equivalent to the Confucius Institutes. Of course, since Japan's national strategy is to build a cultural polity, there is no need for it to emulate the strategy of a newly industrialized country. But viewed from the perspective of Japan's emphasis on culture, and in light of the wants and needs of the ASEAN nations, there is a need, I feel, to establish Japanese language schools abroad. To do this, however, government funds must be available on a long-term basis. Without such a long-term strategy it will be impossible to realize the goal of building schools in Asia.

4

To the Japanese
of the 21st Century

Asia and Japan

Japan as a Cultural Polity

As a nation with a highly developed culture, Japan has adopted many things from abroad, tested them, incorporated and enhanced them. This has been called "East–West eclecticism" or "Japanese spirit with Western technology," but even in the case of technology, Japan did not simply copy and reproduce uncritically. Rather it has combined this technology and know-how with traditional Japanese ways of thought, spirituality, and culture, enhancing and improving where possible on the original. This ability has long been one of the strengths of Japan.

The question then is what Japan's future path should be. In my opinion, Japan should not just be an economic power but should also play a role in the world as a cultural and artistic force. In other words, Japan should actively promote the best of its cultural legacy to the world.

However, this should not be done in the manner of a monotheistic religion, forcing one's values unilaterally on others, but should start with spreading Prince Shotoku's "spirit of harmony." What is important here is that the various countries of the world should respect one another, seeing differences as differences and recognizing dissimilarities as dissimilarities. Moreover, this should not be a simple tolerance of multiplicity but include learning from one another, building connections, and developing new value systems. In this endeavor, Japan's principle of Japanese spirit with Western technology should prove to be useful.

East Asian Nationalism

However, despite our best intentions, it is unfortunately true that not all countries will greet this undertaking with open arms. For instance, in China anti-Japanese sentiment and feelings of enmity are regrettably on the rise. Japanese businesses have been attacked and damaged, and documentaries are still being shown in China on the war with Japan.

China has recently begun to lodge protests when government officials visit the Yasukuni Shrine (dedicated to Japanese war dead, including those condemned as war criminals by the Tokyo Tribunal). China did not protest when the visits first started, and until around 1984 it did not lodge protests even when the prime minister of the day visited the shrine. At a later point in time, however, China decided to protest. I do not know what the political meaning of this is for the Chinese government, but I think that it is unfortunate.

Anti-Japanese sentiment and feelings of enmity are also growing in South Korea. Next year Korean Americans are planning to build a World War II Pacific War Memorial Hall in San Francisco. Korean Americans have also erected memorials to Korean comfort women in five locations in the United States. Considering future relations between Japan and South Korea, these events are difficult to view in a positive light.

Given the present situation, it may be a little difficult to create deeper mutual understanding and goodwill between Japan and China and Korea, but the goal of Japan continues to be peaceful relations and the mutual prosperity of the three countries, coexisting in harmony.

Reassessing the Tokyo War Crimes Tribunal from an Indian Perspective

The discord in relations with China and South Korea results from differences in the "understanding of history." This issue must be resolved from a long-term perspective. One possible means is the reassessment of the Tokyo War Crimes Tribunal.

On my recent visit to India I had the opportunity to meet the grandsons of the Indian jurist Radhabinod Pal and the Indian nationalist Subhas Chandra Bose. At that meeting I agreed to join them in an Indian–Japanese project for the evaluation of history.

Pal was the Indian jurist who at the time of the Tokyo

Tribunal denied the legitimacy of the trials. He argued that the Tribunal contravened the legal principle that a law cannot be applied retrospectively. According to this principle, a law can be applied only to crimes committed after the law becomes effective. Since the Tokyo Tribunal had created new laws against committing crimes against peace and humanity and then applied them ex post facto, he argued that the Tribunal lacked legitimacy. He further believed that if Japanese atrocities were to be judged, then the dropping of atom bombs on Hiroshima and Nagasaki should also be judged.

Subhas Chandra Bose is considered one of the fathers of the nation along with Mahatma Gandhi. While Gandhi attempted to free India from colonialism through nonviolent means, Bose fought alongside Japanese troops in the Imphal Campaign in order to gain independence from the British. As a result, in India, Japan is not viewed as an evil invader but as a welcome liberator. During my stay in India, on August 6, a memorial service was held in the Indian parliament to mark the bombings of Hiroshima and Nagasaki.

How then does the postwar Tokyo Tribunal appear to the eyes of modern Indians? Naturally, I do not wish to deny that Japan had embarked on a war of invasion. It is also true that Japan invaded many Southeast Asian countries. Even now there are many in Singapore and Malaysia who have bitter memories of that time. However, I think that it is also important that the history of this period should not be assessed solely from the viewpoint of the victors but from a variety of differing perspectives.

That is why I would like India and other third-party countries to verify the history of World War II and the Tokyo War Crimes Tribunal. The Indian side seemed eager to join in this project, and so in several years' time I expect to see a report on the meaning of the war and the Tokyo Tribunal. This report will not, of course, be an exercise in rationalization by Japan, but a verification of history by neutral, third-party countries. It should also be significant from the perspective of conveying Japan's principle of coexistence to the world, and in bringing peace and stability to East Asia.

Is Asian Integration Possible?

From the viewpoint of Asian peace and stability, it would be best if Asia were united. The fact is, however, Asia cannot achieve unity as easily as the EU has. Countless hurdles must first be cleared. The first of these hurdles will have been overcome in 2015 with the birth of the ASEAN Economic Community, composed of the 10 countries that make up ASEAN.

In April ASEAN held its 10th meeting of the ASEAN+3 Ministers of Culture and Art in Hue City, Vietnam, which I attended. This 10th meeting was, in fact, the first in which a Japanese Minister of Education participated. This can be taken as an indication that Japan had not, theretofore, paid sufficient attention to ASEAN. Under the Abe administration, however, an ASEAN Summit Meeting was held in Japan at the end of 2014, as part of the strengthening of ties with

ASEAN. I attended the meeting, at which culture was to be emphasized, as the first Japanese Minister of Education to do so, and thus the first ASEAN Ministers of Culture and Arts meeting to be held in Japan came into being. When the meeting was convened, I was surprised to learn that it had previously been held three times in China and twice in South Korea, and that Japan was a latecomer.

Attending the meeting of ministers responsible for culture and the arts, I not only strongly felt the high expectations that the ASEAN countries had for Japan but also sensed a good deal of pro-Japanese sentiment. I came to the conclusion that, not only in the field of culture but also in education and technology, the needs of each ASEAN country should be addressed on an individual basis.

The time when all Asian countries can become close friends may be some way off, but as a first strategic step Japan and the ASEAN countries need to build stronger ties. In the area of trade, Japanese companies should not take the attitude that all is well if their goods sell well, but should build a win-win relationship that promotes the vitality of ASEAN markets. Eschewing narrow nationalism, Japan should continue its present broadminded policy of coexistence.

2,000 Years of Japan–China Relations

Looking back, we can see that Japan and China relations for the last 150 years have been bitter. Before that, however, the two countries had almost 2,000 long years of friendly relations. The 150 traumatic years were a result of Japan's response to Asian incursion by the West and its attempt to join the world's great powers. This was a terrible time for Asian countries, but it is now a part of the past. It is now time, I believe, to reflect on the previous two millennia of amicable relations.

During those 2,000 years Japan and China enjoyed profound cultural exchange. In Japanese art galleries and museums the cultural artifacts of those years can still be seen. Looking back on those good times, the two countries should make a greater effort to repair their friendship. This may take a while, but it is something that is called for by the broader flow of history.

Preparing for the Tokyo Olympics

Sports and the "Way"

The perfect opportunity for Japan to showcase its culture to the world will come in 2020: the Tokyo Olympics and Paralympics.

Just recently a member of the Uruguay International Olympic Committee (IOC) told me that he hoped the 2020 Olympics and Paralympics would be something unique, and he was confident Japan was up to the task. The reason he gave for saying this was simple: he had just read Miyamoto Musashi's *Book of Five Rings*. Musashi (1584–1645) is said to have been Japan's greatest swordsman, but he did not look upon sword fighting as simply a way of killing people; rather he elevated it to an art of living, to a "way" or path (a *michi* or *do*) to a well-lived life. So it was not simply "sword fighting" but the "way of sword fighting" or kendo. The same is true of judo, kyudo (Japanese archery), and others. Japanese think of sports not as a type of competition but as a "way" to living a better life. That is what the man from Uruguay was referring to.

When you think about it, it is true that while there is a method of combat called Brazilian jujutsu there is not one called Brazilian judo. The difference here is between *jutsu* (technique) and *do* (way or path). Overseas, a method of combat is a technique to fight better. In Japan, on the other hand, this technique is elevated to a "way" or "path" to living a more human life. This applies not only to the martial arts (*budo*) but to the way of flower arranging, the way of tea, and other fields in which the goal is the perfection of the practitioner as a human being. I think that this may be unique to Japan.

The Olympic Spirit and Japan

Reading the Olympic Charter, I discovered that the Olympic spirit is very similar to the Japanese way of thinking. According to the Charter, the Olympic spirit calls for athletes not simply to compete in sports, but through sports to find a way of living more harmoniously with one's fellow human beings. The problem is, in previous Olympics and Paralympics, this spirit has not always been realized. If it were possible to realize the Olympic spirit, the member of the Uruguay IOC seemed to be saying, Japan would be the place to do it. The Olympics would be the perfect venue, I realized, for making the Japanese concept of *do* more widely known. But this would not miraculously happen at the Olympics itself, but would have to be the result of careful preparation.

I am currently the President of the Organizing Committee for the Olympic Games in Tokyo, and I hope that Japan will win a historic number of medals. At the same time, through the program Sport for Tomorrow, Japan plans to promote sports around the world by sending coaches to train more than 10 million people in over 100 countries. By doing this, the level of sports in these countries will be raised, making it all the more difficult for Japan to compete successfully in the Olympics. This might be taken as rendering aid to the enemy, and would be unthinkable from a narrow nationalistic point of view. However, this raising of sports to a higher level can also be seen as a manifestation of the Japanese sporting spirit.

Heretofore the Olympics has often been a cut-throat competition between nations for medals, involving fraud and doping, and has thus deviated from the Charter. I would like to see the Olympics turn to the Japanese idea of sports as a way or path to a higher humanity, to a place where the best of humankind is brought out and spiritual growth takes place.

Ichiro and the Japanese Spirit of Sports

As an example of what a "way" or "path" means in sports, I would like to take a look at the baseball player Ichiro Suzuki, who is a perfect embodiment of this way of thinking. In the season before he got his 262nd hit and broke the Major League record for hits in a single season, Ichiro was struggling against the Athletics pitcher Tim Hudson. In an interview Ichiro was asked if Hudson was someone he would rather not face. Ichiro answered that, no, Hudson was the type of great pitcher who brought out the hidden potential in him. He said he wanted to work harder and become the kind of great batter who would bring out the hidden potential in Hudson. This is a perfect example of the Japanese attitude toward sports. When one meets one's match or a formidable rival, it never crosses one's mind to give up or to avoid confrontation. This is alluded to in the Japanese phrase *sessatakuma*, which essentially means to improve oneself through friendly rivalry. This notion lies at the center of Japanese thinking about sports: two parties perfecting themselves through competition with a worthy rival.

Another interview with Ichiro, conducted after he broke

the record, remains fixed in my mind. When he was asked what his next goal would be, I imagine a good many Japanese expected him to say that it was to hit 400. But that is not what he said. What he said was that if he was batting 400 and had reached the required number of plate appearances with only 10 more at-bats remaining, he might not want to stand in the batter's box anymore. Ichiro had started playing baseball because he loved batting, and he hated to think that a situation might arise when he was reluctant to take his turn at bat. In other words, sports for Ichiro is the "way" of bettering himself, not of standing still. He went on to say that he really wanted to improve as a player, but the realm he was now entering was one that could not be expressed in numbers, a world known only to himself. This is a perfect expression of the Japanese notion of "the way." It is not a matter of just winning or just producing great numbers; there is a deeper, more profound world there. By working hard, Ichiro wants to fathom that world and raise himself to the highest level possible. That is the way Ichiro thinks. And this is how the Japanese view sports—it is not just a matter of defeating one's opponent; it is a means of bringing out the hidden potential in one another, of raising one another's level, of mutually growing and maturing. In my mind, sports is the ultimate means of achieving growth as a human being.

Shinto and Japanese Sports

Underlying this Japanese view of sports is surely a Shintoist influence. This refers not to an omnipotent god residing in heaven but to the divine presence that resides in each human being. Thus, when we strive to reach the heights of human potential, we feel we are approaching something divine, that through unrelenting effort we are entering the realm of the sublime. In actual fact, when we watch a first-class athlete in action, we occasionally feel something otherworldly, as if the athlete were possessed by a divine presence. In that sense, what Japanese athletes try to achieve through sports is that feeling of divinity. To think exclusively of how one can best win, to hope that one's opponent suffers a mishap, to think only of oneself—all this goes against the idea of living a life filled with a divine presence. This, I believe, is the type of thinking that forms the bedrock of the Japanese spirit.

Why Are the Olympics so Enthralling?

One more underlying principle of Japanese thought is the "host and guest are one" concept. This means that oneself (the host) and the other (the guest) are not, in fact, two entities, but one. Further, it means that a divine presence resides in both parties, and that by pursuing an ascetic life of spiritual training this divine presence can become manifest. This ascetic training can be pursued through religious practice, through work, or through sports. This is the meaning of a "way" of life.

In the midst of such practice, we may on occasion see or experience a moment of divine possession. In baseball terms, we might say, "That game-ending throw to home plate was otherworldly." This is all a part of the "way," a moment in the presence of something extraordinary, a divinely inspired moment of oneness. All true professionals, regardless of field, have probably experienced such moments at one time or another. And once this has happened, the professional in question invariably becomes more engrossed in his chosen "way." Of course, since we are all finite human beings, there is no way that we can become deities ourselves, but we can catch glimpses of the divine world. And with each such experience, we grow closer to divinity and feel ever more joy in the "way."

Now the question is, why do we feel so moved when watching Olympic and Paralympic events? What is it about seeing top athletes in action that so enthralls us? It is precisely because at the very moment these athletes go beyond normal human limitations, they seem almost as if they were gods. It is this god-like moment that captures the heart of the average person. It is at this moment that world-level athletes appear utterly beautiful, magnificent, and almost divine. It is this that moves us, the superlative sight of a human at the limits of what is humanly possible.

One's Rival as a Mirror of Oneself

As already mentioned above, Japan's sports philosophy places ultimate value not on defeating one's opponent but on the mutual growth that results from competing with a rival. This is true not only of sports but also of daily life and work. The mirror symbolizes this.

The subject of mirrors was mentioned earlier in relation to Kumano Shrine. The Japanese people think of their rival in sports, or the customer in business, as being a mirror image of their self. When looking into a mirror, what appears is a reflection of one's ego. And if that ego is steadily contemplated, it coalesces and assumes a clear form. It is then that the mirror becomes a deity.

In regard to judo, the lyrics of a certain song contain the following: "Don't think of winning; if you do, you will surely lose." To think of winning is a sign that the ego is still at work. As long as your ego is still thinking of winning, you are not in the zone. In such a mental state, frankly it is better to lose. That is the Japanese philosophy of sports. That is why an athlete who is in the zone is said to be "without ego, in a trance" or "of one mind, no distractions." If you reach that state, you will suddenly find that victory is yours. This is the realm of the "way."

A Chance to Showcase the Best of Japan

Here I would like to share one more episode from my trip to India. Speaking in front of a crowd of participants, an Indian official stated that when watching the Soccer World Cup he realized what a special country Japan is. After the match was over, the Japanese fans began cleaning up the stands. He said that this was the first time he had ever seen such a thing; that it was surely a manifestation of the Japanese spirit.

This incident was covered by media around the world, not to mention Japan, and I was not only highly pleased by the favorable reaction of the Indian official but also surprised. These fans were not thinking of how they would be perceived in the eyes of the world, but were simply doing what came naturally to them. And yet, the world was watching. At the 2020 Tokyo Olympics, which after all is being hosted by Japan, I would like to see each and every citizen do such seemingly trivial but meaningful things in the course of their daily life. I hope to make Tokyo that kind of Olympics.

In any case, the Tokyo Olympics and Paralympics are an ideal opportunity not only for athletes but for all Japanese to send a message of goodwill to the world. It is our mission to make use of this chance to contribute positively to global society.

Replacing Nuclear Energy

At the time Tokyo was in the process of being selected as the site of the 2020 Olympics, what the world was then focused on was the Fukushima nuclear disaster. Fukushima is not only a catastrophic environmental disaster but also a grave spiritual issue, one which demands, in accordance with Shinto principles, the immediate discontinuance of nuclear energy. It only stands to reason that if human beings cannot properly manage a source of energy, a different source should be found to replace it. Radioactive waste from these power plants has to be safely stored for over 100,000 years. That is a grave responsibility.

However, as a politician, I believe it would be unrealistic to immediately shut down all nuclear reactors. In order to do so, a considerable span of time would be needed to ready

alternative sources and set up means of production and distribution. In the meantime, the economy would weaken and decline, leading to the hollowing of the country as a whole. Without a realistic agenda for implementing alternative sources of electricity, nuclear power is indispensable. Thus, the only viable political option is to restart the now shuttered reactors as soon as their safety has been verified.

On the other hand, however, the Fukushima Daiichi nuclear disaster could be taken as a divine message to the Japanese people to develop new sources of energy with utmost urgency: renewable energy, natural energy, and "new" energy. Such an undertaking would not only benefit the Japanese people but be a contribution to global society. In fact, this could be said to be Japan's global mission in the field of science and technology. In the field of atmospheric and environmental pollution, Japan has a duty as an advanced country to provide technological assistance to the global community, starting with the developing countries.

When people come from abroad to see the Tokyo Olympics, we would like them to return home with the impression of Tokyo as not only a city that embodies the latest in cutting-edge technology but also a city full of luscious greenery, clean rivers, and a beautiful ocean. At the same time, we would like to impress upon these visitors the importance of resolving environmental issues. After all, the pollution of the environment is not exclusively a Japanese problem; it is a problem for all humankind. This is precisely why Japan must strive even harder in the creation of technological environmental solutions.

A Society for the Young and Old, Men and Women

THE SPEED OF POPULATION DECLINE IS THE ISSUE

In discussing the future of Japan, we have to consider the impact of aging and the falling birthrate. By 2030 25% of the total population will be over 60, and by 2060 40%. I myself, however, am not so pessimistic about the shrinking of the population. At the beginning of the Meiji period, about 150 years ago, the population stood at only 40 million in comparison to the present 126 million. And about 300 years ago, in the Edo period, it was a mere 30 million. Given the rapid and massive increases in the population after World War II, it is possible to argue that the present decline is actually only a return to a former state.

In the midst of a rapidly shrinking society, the problem is how the country is to support its senior citizens. If the decline were gradual, the burden on society would not be so great, but with rapid shrinkage the issue is how to create the businesses that will support the lives of the elderly. Even if the population should be halved and a great many local governments disappear, that could be dealt with. The problem is that with precipitous shrinkage, local government will cease to function. Over a 300-year span, adjustments could be made, but a rapid decrease creates problems of prodigious proportions.

Rebuilding the Japanese Economy through Education

The issue of an aging and low-birth-rate society can be approached in a number of ways, but the one I place my greatest hopes on is education.

Education is a prerequisite for the improvement of the lives of each and every citizen. It increases the added value of every person. It can improve the productivity of each worker, so that someone who has an annual income of ¥4 million can raise that to ¥8 million. This is not a matter of hours worked. It is not realistic for someone who is working 8 hours a day to increase that to 16 and double their income. What has to be increased is not the quantity of work but its quality. In other words, it is education that allows people to get higher value-added employment.

According to statistics, people without a good education are less likely to marry, and even if they do, they are less likely to have more than one child. In essence, they are unable to find work to support a family. Further, children of low-income families are less likely to attend high school or college. The reality is that children of impoverished families, relatively speaking, have no future. One of the reasons for this is the way education is paid for in Japan. In Japan the costs of education are borne by the family. In the developed world, educational costs are generally borne by the state. Japan must rectify this situation. We as a nation have to recognize that all citizens have a right to education, and we must create the conditions that enable all Japanese to take advantage of this right. It is education that is the key to creating a flatter society.

New Workforces for a Shrinking Society

The most well-paid sector of the Japanese workforce is largely made up of men between the ages of 18 to 65. Of late, however, more attention is being paid to the development of the female workforce. Currently, even if a woman finishes higher levels of education, once she marries and has children, the only work available to her after raising her children is non-regular employment in part-time and temporary jobs. This is not realizing the potential of the female population. What can be done to rectify this situation? One possibility is for women to re-enter college or attend graduate school and augment their present capabilities. Of course, this requires an educational framework that realizes women's hidden potential over the full course of their working lives. This is precisely the framework that must be built.

Another potential labor force I consider particularly important is the elderly. People of my age are now approaching retirement. They still have the ability to work, but immediately after retirement many of them prefer not to. With a substantial retirement bonus, they can live comfortably for two or three years. For society this is a loss. Conversely, older people could make use of their many years of experience by becoming instructors, or they could re-enter college or other educational institutions and undertake new challenges in life. In 2014 the Ministry of Education started a Saturday Education program that encourages retired corporate employees to become instructors in the educational system. In the coming era, we need to build an environment in which, given good health and the will to work, people in their 70s or 80s should be able to continue working. This can also provide the elderly with new meaning to life.

Through education I believe it is possible to create many of the factors required for economic growth. If nothing is done now, the future may be bleak, but if done now, it is not too late. From here on, the population of Japan will continue to dwindle. However, I think it is still perfectly possible to build a society that can withstand a declining population. What is needed is a social framework in which, through education, all members are participants.

A Multiple Career Friendly Society

Japan has developed by accepting a diverse number of foreign influences, but it still lags behind other countries in providing working opportunities for women and the elderly. There are many cases of women at the peak of their working lives who become homemakers after having children, and the problem facing us now is how to provide working opportunities for capable women who want to re-enter the workforce after their children have grown up. At present, once women or even middle-aged men leave the company they work for, it is very difficult to find good employment again. Providing work opportunities for such people is an important issue that must be resolved.

Of course, the raising of children is extraordinarily creative work in itself. There can surely be no more rewarding work than this. After all, you are bringing up a child who possesses almost unlimited possibilities. Children are, in a sense, like little gods. Thus, while being aware that raising children is a wonderful thing in itself, provision should be made for those women who have the capability, the desire, and the will to re-enter the workforce. In other words, it is important that women should be able to choose between supporting the family at home or working outside the home. Ideally, we should be able to accommodate everyone, regardless of sex, through the different stages of their lives—the stage when they concentrate on the home, the stage when they concentrate on work, the educational stage when they prepare for the next step forward, and so forth.

Acceptance of Immigrants Only a Matter of Time

With aging and low birthrates accelerating, the acceptance of immigrants into Japan is surely only a matter of time. Since Japan is not a closed country, it is only natural that there be more immigration from abroad. However, a rapid and massive influx could lead to cultural breakdown, which is why the process should be slow and measured. This is also why, at the beginning, only the most qualified should be selected for admittance. An unselected, massive deluge of immigrants could lead to irreparable damage to Japanese society.

While some restrictions on immigration are unavoidable, what must be eschewed is discrimination in the workplace and daily life. Japanese culture has a long tradition of recognizing individual worth. For example, in passing in the corridor, a company president might casually thank a cleaner for their good work, treating the cleaner as he would any other worker or member of the group. On the other hand, when I hear people say that immigrants are not Japanese and do not have to be treated the same, it makes me a little sad. What is important in the issue of immigration is not just system and organization, but what it is that brought Japanese and immigrants together to work as a team. What is important, regardless of differences in the type of work done, is whether people can feel that it is meaningful to work together, whether they want to grow and mature together. This applies to Japanese people as well. In managing the workplace, it is important for everyone to be treated equally, even though some of the Japanese may be non-regular workers and others regular employees. Without this type of management, the workplace atmosphere deteriorates.

Traditionally, Japanese management has made no distinctions with regard to academic background, title, or managerial position. The core philosophy holds that all employees are essential to the success of the company. In the past not a few managers had the experience of meeting employees who had the words of the Buddhist priest Saicho (767–822) ingrained in their minds: "Shine a light on one corner of the world, and you are a national treasure." Likewise, true Japanese management makes no distinction between race or nationality.

Unfortunately, the recent incursions of Western financial capitalism have led to a retrenchment in this type of Japanese management. In the near future, when the number of immigrants has increased, if there should be discrimination in the workplace, this could be viewed as the destruction of what was once an exemplary aspect of Japanese culture.

As mentioned earlier, when I met former Prime Minister Mahathir, I told him that I often hear people say that "Japan of 30 or 40 years ago was superlative in many ways, but now it seems to have lost all that." Sometimes I myself feel that Japanese culture is under threat. That is why, here and now, it is time for the Japanese to return to their roots. What was once admirable about Japan has to be closely reexamined.

The Importance of Education with a Social Purpose

One of the remarkable features of traditional Japanese culture was the scope and depth of its work ethic. Japanese firms place great emphasis on the meaningfulness of work for each individual in the workplace. Before the meaningfulness of work, of course, comes the quality of life. It is vital, I think, to revive the importance that traditional Japan placed on these two aspects of life.

What, then, should be done to see that young Japanese feel the meaningfulness of work and life? What is important here, I believe, is education with a social purpose.

"Purpose" here does not mean a "dream." A dream is a personal thing, but a social purpose is a commitment by the individual to doing something for the good of society. This type of goal does not begin and end with the individual. It always has reference to society; it refers to a life that elevates society or other people, a life with a greater than personal aim. This is exactly what the coming Japan is in need of: education that teaches social purpose.

In so far as a social purpose is a commitment to contributing to society, it cannot be done in isolation. Purpose is realized when people come together, when they feel a positive response, become friends, comrades, and combine their efforts. This process starts from the moment when a social purpose is embraced.

As it happens, people with social purpose naturally

attract intangible or cultural capital. Other people come forward with helpful advice, offer their time on a gratis basis, and introduce useful connections; that is, a voluntary economy comes into being.

Furthermore, social purpose cannot always be achieved in a single generation. In fact, the higher the purpose, the greater the possibility that it will not be accomplished within the scope of a single lifetime. For instance, if we were to commit to solving the problem of global warming, this goal could only be achieved over the course of several generations. Thus, if we have high goals, we must give it our all during our time on this planet, and then pass it on to the next generation with our prayers for their success.

Who Implements Social Purpose?

At its deepest level, education with a social purpose entails the question of who gets credit for successfully accomplishing its lofty goals.

Pertinent here is the Japanese maxim, "What I have accomplished is not my own." Even should a person achieve great things in his lifetime, he will not say, "I did that all by myself, without any help." Rather, our sage ancestors almost invariably said, "What I have accomplished was done by heaven. It was heaven working through me." We still have much to learn from the wisdom of our forefathers.

Moreover, if we approach life with this attitude—"What

I have accomplished is not my own"—we miraculously find that, through the dispensation of heaven, we are blessed by encounters with many likeminded people. We find ourselves leading a life directed by something larger than ourselves.

Behind social purpose is another important concept—mission. This pair of principles is of vital importance in leading a fulfilling life. What then is "mission"?

The word for mission in Japanese is *shimei*. It is written with two Chinese characters that can be literally read as "using one's life." My life is the span of time granted by heaven. It will one day come to an end, but we know not when. How will we "use" this precious life, this invaluable gift? That resolution is a sense of mission, social purpose.

A society in which all Japanese embrace social purpose and a sense of mission—that would be a wonderful achievement. With all my heart I hope that Japan will create such a society in the 21st century.

Postscript

Now, in the 21st century, freedom of employment is taken for granted around the world. But this is a recent freedom when seen against the backdrop of history. In Japan, for example, until just 150 years ago the son of a farmer was a farmer for life, the son of a samurai a samurai for life.

In modern times, however, it became possible to become anything you desired to be, provided you had the will and the ability. The arrival of democracy granted opportunity and possibility to everyone. In the 21st century, however, one American economist projects that the next 30 years will be an age of unprecedented change, an age in which 65% of all occupations existing today will disappear.

As indicated by the previously mentioned survey stating that 84% of first-year high school students considered themselves losers, the present day gives everyone a chance for advancement but it also puts everyone at risk, producing a social environment replete with stress.

This is precisely why it is necessary to ask yourself why

you were born, what your purpose in life is, and to think hard about your identity.

Perhaps the reason you were born in this world was to be of service to society, to your family, or to your country. To know the answer to this question, it is necessary to know your roots. The more you learn, the more you will know about your real self, and the more you will recognize the good in others.

In order to study and fathom the various problems facing the 21st century, Japan is a good place to start, but why? Simply because it is a good yardstick. For instance, Japan is not imbued with one religious doctrine; neither is it socially regulated by one political ideology. Japan takes the best in thought, philosophy, and religion from other countries. Flexible and with low resistance to change, it provides the opportunity for the formation of a new civilization. This is not to suggest the superiority of Japanese culture, but rather it is a matter of historical necessity. In learning more about Japanese culture, history, and tradition, the Japanese themselves have to pass on what they have learned to the world in a multilayered manner. I would be pleased if this book can make a small contribution to that endeavor.

In conclusion, I would like to express my appreciation to the following people for their contribution to the writing of this book: Hiroshi Tasaka, Kumi Fujisawa, Kuniaki Ura, Katsuhiko Mizuno, Shuku Onodera, Atsuo Yamamoto, and Shiomi Kaneda.

Hakubun Shimomura
November 2015

About Hakubun Shimomura

Diet Member (House of Representatives)

Deputy Secretary-General for Special Missions

Special Advisor to the President

Former Minister of Education, Culture, Sports, Science, and Technology

Former President of the Organizing Committee for the Olympic Games

Born in 1954 in Gunma Prefecture, Japan.

Graduated from the Department of Education, Waseda University.

Elected to the Tokyo Metropolitan Assembly in 1989 and served two terms over seven years.

In 1996 he was elected to the Lower House of the Diet from the Tokyo No. 11 district and is now in his seventh term. When nine, the sudden death of his father in an automobile accident led to financial hardship for the family. He managed to graduate from high school and university with the help of scholarships. During that time he began to feel the need to reciprocate the kindness he had been shown. Through his role as head of the Waseda University debating society, he became acquainted with many passionate people who went on to lead Japan. It was then that he determined that his future role in life was to become a politician. Subsequently, with this sense of mission as a driving force he has been active in restructuring Japan through education. In the first Shinzo Abe administration he served as deputy chief cabinet secretary, and in the second and third cabinets as the Minister of Education, Minister in Charge of Education Rebuilding, and President of the Organizing Committee for the Olympic Games.

His principal publications are *Kyōiku gekihen* (Radical Change in Education), Meiseisha; *Gakkō o kaeru "kyōiku tokku": Kodomo to Nihon no shōrai o ninaeru ka* (School-Changing "Special Education Districts": Can They Change the Future of Japan and Its Children?), Omura Shoten; *Kosodate hissu manyuaru* (The Essential Childrearing Manual), Human; *Juku sono ari no mama no sugata* (Cram Schools as They Are), Gakuyo Shobo; *Satchā kaikaku ni manabu kyōiku seijōka e no michi* (The Road to Educational Normalization as Learned from the Thatcher Revolution), PHP Institute; *Shimomura Hakubun no kyōiku rikkokuron* (The Rebuilding of Japan through Education according to Shimomura Hakubun), Kawade Shobo Shinsha; and *Kyūsai de chichi o nakushita shimbun-haitatsu shōnen kara monbu daijin ni* (From Newspaper Delivery Boy who Lost his Father to the Minister of Education), Kairyusha.

Hakubun Shimomura's official website can be found at http://www.hakubun.biz/.

The Culture of Japan as a New Global Value
世界を照らす日本のこころ［英文版］

2016年2月2日　第1刷発行

著　者　　下村博文

翻　訳　　マイケル・ブレーズ

発行者　　浦　晋亮

発行所　　IBC パブリッシング株式会社
　　　　　〒162-0804 東京都新宿区中里町29番3号 菱秀神楽坂ビル9F
　　　　　Tel. 03-3513-4511　Fax. 03-3513-4512
　　　　　www.ibcpub.co.jp

印刷所　　株式会社シナノパブリッシングプレス

© Hakubun Shimomura, IBC Publishing Inc. 2016
Printed in Japan

落丁本・乱丁本は、小社宛にお送りください。送料小社負担にてお取り替えいたします。
本書の無断複写（コピー）は著作権法上での例外を除き禁じられています。

ISBN978-4-7946-0374-6 C0082